HOLIDAY COOKIES

PRIZE-WINNING
FAMILY RECIPES FROM THE

Chicago Tribune

FOR

**COOKIES
BARS
BROWNIES**

AND MORE

S

SURREY
BOOKS

AN **AGATE** IMPRINT

CHICAGO

Chicago Tribune

Tony W. Hunter, CEO & Publisher
Gerould W. Kern, Senior Vice President, Editor
Bill Adee, Executive Vice President/Digital
Joycelyn Winnecke, Vice President, Associate Editor
Jane Hirt, Vice President, Managing Editor
Peter Kendall, Deputy Managing Editor

Printed in China.

Library of Congress Cataloging-in-Publication Data
Holiday cookies (Chicago, Ill.)
 Holiday cookies : prize-winning family recipes from the Chicago Tribune for cookies, bars, brownies and more.
    pages cm
 Includes index.
 Summary: "A collection of recipes from the Chicago Tribune's annual holiday cookie contest"-- Provided by publisher.
 ISBN 978-1-57284-164-2 (hard cover) -- ISBN 1-57284-164-8 (hard cover)
1. Cookies. 2. Holiday cooking. I. Chicago Tribune (Firm) II. Title.
 TX772.H65 2014
 641.86'54--dc23
                                2014026785

10 9 8 7 6 5 4 3 2

Surrey is an imprint of Agate Publishing. Agate books are available in bulk at discount prices. For more information visit agatepublishing.com.

ABOUT THIS BOOK

The recipes in this book were selected from the history of the
Chicago Tribune's Holiday Cookie Contest. For this contest,
readers submit both a recipe and a brief essay describing what
made the cookie special to the writer. The Chicago Tribune
considers these essays while choosing the finalists.

106

79

23

162

42

144

CONTENTS

INTRODUCTION
by **Carol Mighton Haddix**

Every December, my grandmother would send a box to us.
We knew what it was, and the anticipation we children had was palpable as we tore off the plain brown paper wrapping. Inside was an array of Christmas cookies, each individually nestled in wax paper. After more unwrapping, we would arrange the cookies on a platter: Swedish spritz, brown-eyed Susans, date-nut bars, decorated sugar cookies, and walnut refrigerator cookies. The selection was the same each year, and we adored them. Mom had to really work to make sure we didn't sneak more than one or two at a time. The box marked the beginning of the holiday season. It was filled with magic and memories, and it was a joyful link to our far-away grandparents.

This scene is repeated in homes across the country as the winter holidays approach, whether it is Christmas, Hanukkah, or Kwanzaa. As homemade treasures, cookies mark a season of symbolic traditions. And each cookie has a story, as we have learned through the years of running Good Eating's Holiday Cookie Contest. Started in 1986, this Chicago Tribune contest asks readers for their favorite cookie recipes. The contest rules may have changed slightly from year to year, but, in essence, we require an essay from contestants as well as the recipe. We ask them: What makes this cookie special? What does it mean to you and your family? And they respond with hundreds of stories each year.

The contest has become very popular. We learned just how popular one year, when in a misguided quest to run something different in the food section in early December, we

Hazelnut Espresso Truffle Cookies (p. 170)

decided to skip the competition. Readers complained in force. They wanted the contest back! Where were the cookie recipes? We didn't make that mistake again, and the contest continues to this day.

As the holidays approach each year, cookies begin arriving at the Tribune Tower in all shapes, sizes and flavors. Some seem simple, some fancy. Others are cakey, chewy or crisp. Many feature nuts or chocolate chips, or are layered with preserves. Vanilla, butter, sugar and flour form the basis of most. Ginger, cinnamon, nutmeg, cloves — all of the warm spices of the season are there. But then judges will be surprised by a cookie with more unusual flavorings such as coffee, almond, lemon or rum.

Judging is done by the food and dining staff, and often a professional baker or pastry chef. Believe me, it may be fun, but it's not easy! What judges are looking for never varies: the best-tasting and best-looking cookies of the bunch. Some years, it can be very difficult to choose between a creative, complex cookie and a simple, perfectly executed cookie.

One year, we invited the great Julia Child to help us judge the contest. She was in town to speak at a food conference, and we took the chance and called her. She said she would love to taste some cookies.

But after sampling the finalists' offerings in the test kitchen, she harrumphed in her one-of-a-kind voice: "Well, I wouldn't make *any* of these cookies!" Julia was a tough judge! And she always said what she really thought. She pointed out that some of the bakers had used

We have learned many other cookie-making tips from our expert judges through the years: Follow the recipe exactly. Be patient when shaping and cutting cookies. Be sure not to over-bake cookies. **And sometimes, simple is better.**

less-than-quality ingredients. One cookie had stale nuts, another used low-quality chocolate. The rest of the judges weren't quite as critical, and we did come up with three winners that year.

But Julia had a point. Even though a cookie recipe may have been passed down through generations of cooks, it still needs to be followed with care, using top-notch ingredients.

We have learned many other cookie-making tips from Julia and our expert judges through the years: Follow the recipe exactly. Be patient when shaping and cutting cookies. Be sure not to over-bake cookies (ovens may be different). And sometimes, simple is better.

One of those simple cookie recipes we loved was called Mexican Mice. Caryn Lerner of Vernon Hills, Ill., created her "mice" one year because her nieces and nephews would not eat her traditional Mexican wedding cake cookies. She won second place in the 2000 contest by decorating the cookies with almond ears, chocolate whiskers and chow-mein-noodle tails. They were so cute, we couldn't help but say, "Aw!"

Another favorite, Baba's Cream Cheese Kolacky, came from Emily Dressel's grandmother, who gave her a lesson in how to make the rich, apricot-filled cookie along with some advice: "You just have to sense it, Emily. The dough will tell you what it needs." Emily won first place in 2008.

Other staff favorites included Orange Pecan Ice Box Cookies, Hazelnut Espresso Truffle Cookies, Sparkly Oatmeal Cookies and Laced Cookies. Many more excellent treasures are collected in this book, and perhaps by trying them, you'll find yourself creating new traditions for your family. Maybe one day your grandchildren — with wide-eyed anticipation — will feel the same pleasures of the cookie-loving generations that came before.

Carol Mighton Haddix retired as food editor of the Chicago Tribune in 2011, a post she held for 31 years. She has edited many Tribune cookbooks, including "Good Eating's Best of the Best: Great Recipes of the Past Decade from the Chicago Tribune Test Kitchen" (2011). She also edited and wrote the introduction for "Chicago Cooks: 25 Years of Food History with Menus, Recipes, and Tips from Les Dames d'Escoffier Chicago" (2007). She has judged national and local food competitions and given lectures on Chicago food history.

COOKIES 101

Tips for Success

Homemade cookies often may look simple, but the good ones take know-how culled from long experience in baking. A real cookie maven is Nancy Baggett, who tested almost 30,000 to come up with the recipes for "The All-American Cookie Book" (Houghton Mifflin). Here, adapted from the chapter called "How to Make Great Cookies Every Single Time," are some tips for doing your best work yet in the kitchen:

Measure, don't guess In baking, accuracy really counts. For measuring liquids, use transparent or 1- or 2-cup marked measuring cups. Set the cup on a flat surface. For measuring dry ingredients, graduated cups make it easy to obtain the exact amount needed by leveling off with the sweep of a long-bladed spatula or knife, rather than just judging by sight.

Read (and follow!) directions Prepare the recipe exactly as it is written at least once before making any changes. Pay particular attention to what temperature ingredients should be because this can have a major effect on baking success. Follow the instructions on mixing procedures and the order for adding ingredients.

Beware of substitutions Semisweet chocolate blocks and semisweet chocolate morsels are often not interchangeable. Blocks and morsels were designed for different purposes; manufacturers intend for semisweet chocolate blocks to be used melted, so these generally melt smoothly and are fairly fluid. Chocolate chips are designed to hold their shape when heated, so are usually stiff when melted.

Butter and regular stick margarine are sometimes interchangeable; butter and tub-style, light or diet margarine are never interchangeable.

Granulated sugar and brown sugar are rarely interchangeable. Brown sugar is moister, heavier and coarser than granulated sugar, so it will also change the cookie texture.

Simple Drop Cookies

SIMPLE DROP COOKIES

HOLIDAY COOKIES

No Ingredient Left Behind Cookies

Daniel Barnett credited his son Jake and his son's buddies for helping him fine-tune this recipe, which won an honorable mention in 2007.

¾ cup white flour

¾ cup whole-wheat flour

2 tablespoons flaxseed, ground in a blender to meal

Grated zest of 1 orange

1½ teaspoons cinnamon

1 teaspoon baking soda

½ teaspoon salt

1 rounded teaspoon instant coffee

1 teaspoon vanilla

2 sticks (1 cup) butter, softened

1 cup packed brown sugar

2 eggs

1 cup assorted baking chips and baking candy, see note

¾ cup butterscotch chips

¼ cup chopped chocolate-covered espresso beans

½ cup chopped walnuts

½ cup chopped macadamia nuts

1½ cups quick oats

1½ cups old-fashioned oats

Prep time: 35 minutes

Bake time: 11 minutes per batch

1. Heat the oven to 375 degrees. Stir together the flours, flaxseed, orange zest, cinnamon, baking soda and salt in a large bowl; set aside. Place the instant coffee in a small bowl; add vanilla. Stir until combined; set aside.

2. Cream the butter and brown sugar in a large bowl with a mixer on medium speed until light and creamy, about 3 minutes. Mix in the eggs, 1 at a time, beating until fluffy, about 2 minutes. Stir in the dry ingredients just until mixed. Stir in the chips and espresso beans, dissolved coffee and the nuts. Stir in the oats, 1 cup at a time.

3. Form into rounded 1-inch balls on an ungreased cookie sheet. Bake until firm and light brown, about 11 minutes. Cool on a wire rack.

Note: Mix any of the following: semisweet chocolate, mint, caramel swirl, white chocolate, raspberry, cappuccino or peanut butter chips, or chocolate candy bar bits.

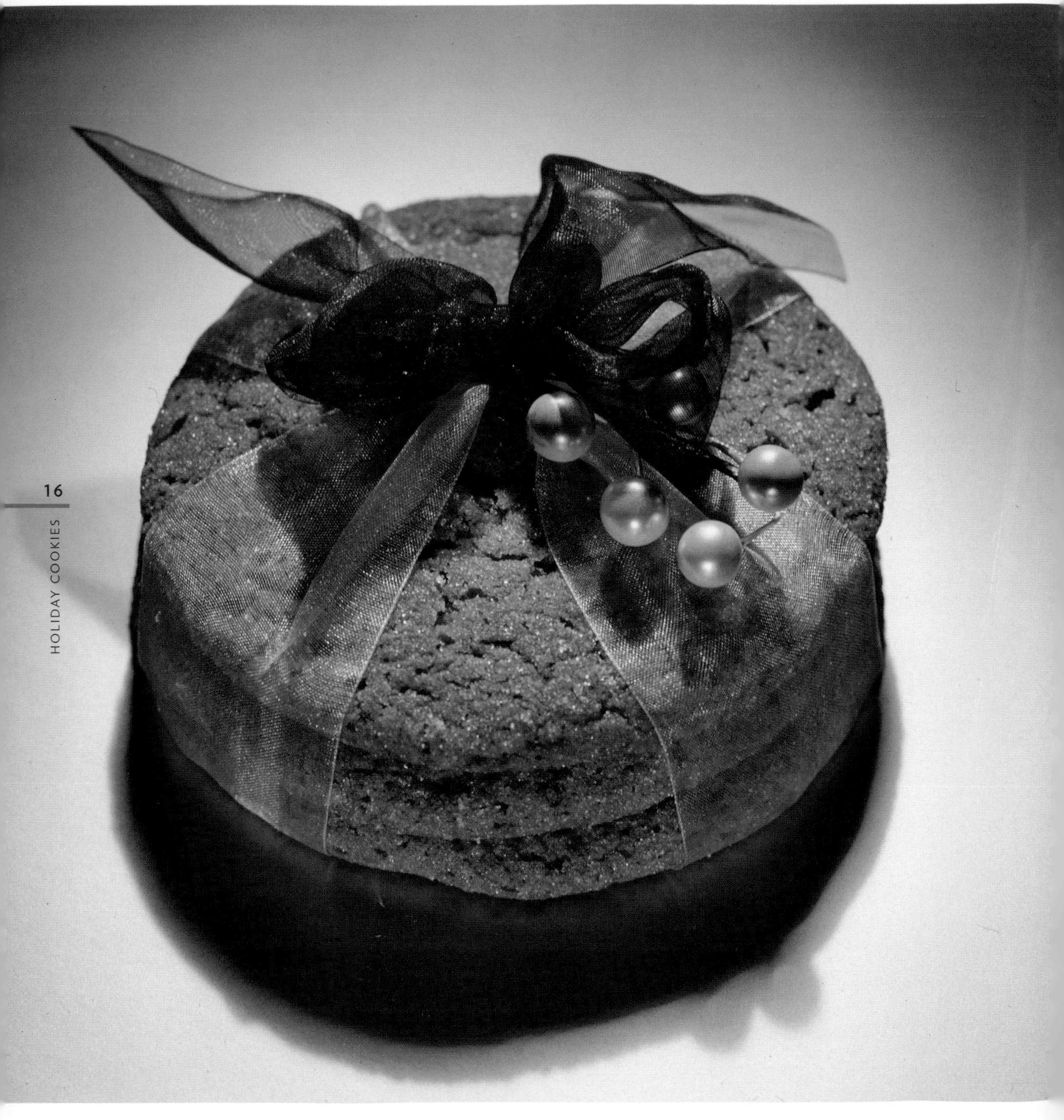

Yield: 10 large or
40 small cookies

2¼   cups unsifted all-purpose
      flour
¾   cup vegetable oil
½   cup sugar
1   large egg
¼   cup pure maple syrup
¼   cup sorghum molasses
2   teaspoons baking soda
1   teaspoon ginger
½   teaspoon cinnamon
½   teaspoon cardamom
¼   teaspoon salt
     Additional sugar for
     coating

Prep time: 20 minutes

Bake time: 10 to 15
minutes per batch

Friendship Cookies

Agnes Da Costa won fourth place for this recipe in the
1995 contest.

1. Heat oven to 350 degrees. Have ungreased baking
sheet(s) ready.

2. Combine all ingredients, except sugar for coating, in
large bowl of an electric mixer. Beat on low speed until
combined. Refrigerate to firm dough slightly, about 20
minutes.

3. Roll into large balls, using ¼ cup dough each for
large cookies or a scant tablespoon for smaller cookies
(dough will be soft). Roll in additional sugar to coat.
Arrange on baking sheet, spacing them 3 inches apart.

4. Bake until set, about 15 minutes for large cookies
and 10 minutes for smaller ones. Cool on baking sheet
1 minute before transferring to wire rack to cool.

Yield: About 3 dozen cookies

Rumprint Cookies

Rebecca Gottfred, 1994 first-place winner, made these cookies with her sister in their annual pre-Christmas baking session. Both of their families declared them a yearly must. The recipe doubles and triples easily, and the baked cookies freeze well.

Dough:

⅔ cup (10⅔ tablespoons) unsalted butter, softened

⅓ cup granulated sugar

1 large egg

1 teaspoon pure vanilla extract

¼ teaspoon salt

1¾ cups all-purpose flour

¼–½ teaspoon nutmeg or to taste

Filling:

¼ cup (½ stick) unsalted butter, softened

1 cup sifted confectioners' sugar

½–1 teaspoon rum extract or to taste

Nutmeg for garnish

 Prep time:
1 hour, 30 minutes

Chill time:
1 hour, 15 minutes

Bake time:
12 minutes per batch

1. Beat butter in large bowl of electric mixer until light; beat in sugar until fluffy. Beat in egg, vanilla and salt; beat well. Stir in flour and nutmeg until well mixed. Refrigerate dough, covered, 1 hour.

2. Heat oven to 350 degrees. Have ungreased baking sheets ready.

3. Shape dough into 1-inch diameter balls. Place 2 inches apart on baking sheets. Press down centers with thumb. Bake until barely golden, about 12 minutes. Cool on wire racks.

4. For filling, beat butter until light. Beat in confectioners' sugar until fluffy. Add rum extract to taste. Beat well. Fill a pastry bag fitted with a medium star tip with the filling. Pipe a star into the center of each cookie. Sprinkle with nutmeg. Chill until filling firms, 15 minutes.

From top: Surprise Packages (p. 146); Kolachkes (p. 83); Rumprint Cookies (opposite)

Springerle

Yield: About 7 dozen
2-inch cookies

Pictured on p. 179

Connie Meisinger's grandmother used to send her springerle packages in the mail, which signaled to her that Christmas was just around the corner. Her grandmother called them "dunkin'" cookies because they were perfect for dipping in coffee. At the 1993 competition, Meisinger, who tied for third, said she started her own tradition of mailing the cookies to her friends and relatives.

½   teaspoon baker's ammonia, see below

2   tablespoons milk

6   large eggs, room temperature

1½   pounds confectioners' sugar, about 6 cups

½   cup (1 stick) unsalted butter, softened

Scant ½ teaspoon anise oil, see note on opposite page

½   teaspoon salt

2   pounds cake flour, sifted, about 8 cups

Prep time: 40 minutes

Standing time: 1 hour, plus overnight

Bake time: 10 to 12 minutes per batch

Aging time:
1 week or more

1. Mash baker's ammonia with a rolling pin if it is not powdered. Dissolve it in the milk in a small bowl and let stand 1 hour before using.

2. Beat eggs in large bowl of electric mixer until thick and lemon-colored, about 5 minutes. Gradually beat in confectioners' sugar until creamy and smooth. Add butter and beat again until creamy. Add anise oil, dissolved baker's ammonia and salt; beat to mix. Gradually beat in enough flour to make a stiff dough.

3. Cut off pieces of dough and work in more flour on a floured work surface until dough is stiff enough to roll out and hold the design of the springerle rolling pin or mold. Roll out on a lightly floured board with a floured rolling pin to ¼-inch thickness. Press design on dough with a floured springerle rolling pin or mold. Cut cookies apart using a floured knife. Leave on work surface covered with a clean kitchen towel overnight.

4. The next day, heat oven to 325 degrees. Bake cookies on greased baking sheets, until barely golden on the bottom, 10 to 12 minutes. Cool on wire racks. Store in tightly covered tins and allow to mellow at least 1 week before serving.

Baker's ammonia: Also known as ammonium bicarbonate, hartshorn, hjortron and hirschorn salz, it is a precursor to modern leavening agents and still used by many European, Greek and Middle Eastern bakers. It is difficult to find and does not store well (the ammonia dissipates readily), so buy it in small quantities and store it in a tightly closed jar.

Note: This recipe also can be made using 1½ teaspoons baking powder (in place of the milk and the baker's ammonia) and anise extract instead of anise oil. However, the cookies will not be as delicately textured and the anise flavor not quite as rich. If using baking powder, add it with the salt to the batter.

"These cookies are a massive chewy delight of chocolate and nuts," said Dr. Lynn Levy, 2010 first-place winner. She's not kidding. "One recipe contains 3 cups of semisweet chocolate chips and a pound of nuts. Each coveted cookie weighs almost a quarter of a pound. Nobody eats an entire cookie for dessert." But you can try.

Yield: 20 cookies

Mrs. Levy's Giant Chocolate Chip Cookies

2 cups firmly packed light brown sugar

2 sticks (1 cup) unsalted butter, room temperature

1 tablespoon vanilla

2 large eggs

2½ cups unsifted flour

1 teaspoon salt

1 teaspoon baking powder

4 cups chopped walnuts

3 cups semisweet chocolate chips

 **Prep time:** 15 minutes

Bake time: 15 minutes per batch

1. Heat oven to 375 degrees. Beat sugar, butter and vanilla in a large bowl with a mixer until light and fluffy. Beat in eggs until lighter. Add flour, salt and baking powder; beat just until mixed. Stir in walnuts and chocolate chips.

2. Drop cookie mixture by ½ cup measure onto greased or parchment-lined baking sheets, leaving plenty of space between. Flatten each cookie slightly with back of fork. Bake until golden, about 15 minutes. Cool on sheet 2 minutes; transfer to a wire rack. Cool completely.

Drommer (Dreamer) Cookies

"A great thing about these little cookies is that they're hard to ruin," wrote 11-year-old Mia Cudecki, adding that her Norwegian grandmother baked these delicate, brown-butter Scandinavian treats for her annual Christmas bake sale. This recipe received an honorable mention in 2006.

2 sticks (1 cup) butter
2 cups flour
1 teaspoon baking powder
¾ cup sugar
2 teaspoons vanilla
36 blanched almond halves

Prep time: 25 minutes
Standing time: 45 minutes

Bake time: 50 minutes per batch

1. Heat oven to 300 degrees. Melt butter in a medium saucepan over low heat, stirring often, until beginning to brown, about 15 minutes. Pour into a large bowl, making sure to add any browned bits from the bottom of the pan; cool completely, about 45 minutes. Meanwhile, stir flour and baking powder together; set aside.

2. Add sugar to browned butter. Beat with a mixer on medium speed until fluffy; beat in vanilla. Blend in flour mixture; beat until just combined. Form into 1-inch balls; transfer to a greased or parchment-lined baking sheet. Press an almond half on top of each cookie to flatten. Bake until cookies begin to brown, 50 minutes.

Yield: 44 cookies

Pictured on p. 112

Hazelnut-Coffee Oatmeal Cookies

Taking third place in the 2004 contest, these cookies from Amy Rodriguez offer a delightful blend of textures and flavors. Rodriguez adapted these cookies from a recipe used by her grandmother, whom she described as fun-loving and young at heart, but meticulous when it came to baking Christmas cookies. Because the heat from just-baked cookies helps melt the chocolate, place the candy squares on the cookies immediately after removing them from the oven.

1½ cups quick or old-fashioned uncooked oats

1 cup flour

1 teaspoon baking soda

1 teaspoon salt

1 stick (½ cup) butter, softened

½ cup brown sugar

½ cup granulated sugar

1 egg

½ teaspoon vanilla

2 tablespoons instant coffee granules

2 tablespoons hazelnut-flavored non-dairy creamer

½ cup chopped nuts

1 chocolate bar (4 ounces), separated into small rectangles

44 pecan halves

Prep time: 20 minutes

Chill time: 30 minutes

Bake time: 10 minutes per batch

1. Pulse oats in food processor 10 times; set aside. Sift together flour, baking soda and salt in a bowl; set aside.

2. Cream butter with a mixer on medium-high speed until smooth. Add sugars, egg and vanilla, beating until smooth. Add coffee granules and non-dairy creamer.

3. Reduce mixer speed to low; add oats and chopped nuts. Stir in flour mixture. Transfer mixture to a bowl; cover with plastic wrap. Refrigerate 30 minutes.

4. Heat oven to 375 degrees. Drop dough by teaspoon onto ungreased cookie sheet. Bake until puffed, cracked on top and slightly brown around the edges, about 10 minutes. Remove cookie sheets from oven. Immediately place a chocolate rectangle on each cookie. Top chocolate with a pecan half. Remove cookie from cookie sheet. Transfer to cooling rack to cool.

Yield: 4½ dozen cookies

Tear-drop Anise Cookies

These pastel-frosted cookies from Jan Moffitt tied for third place in the 1998 contest. "People ask us why we do this," Moffitt wrote. "There's a real easy answer: It isn't about baking cookies, it's about making memories."

Dough:

5 cups all-purpose flour

5 teaspoons baking powder

⅛ teaspoon salt

1½ cups sugar

1 cup (2 sticks) butter, softened

¼ teaspoon anise oil or 1 teaspoon anise extract

6 large eggs

Glaze:

2 cups sifted confectioners' sugar

¼ cup milk

Food coloring

Prep time: 40 minutes

Bake time: 8 to 10 minutes per batch

1. Heat oven to 350 degrees. Whisk together flour, baking powder and salt in large bowl. Set aside. Beat sugar, butter and anise oil in bowl of electric mixer until light and fluffy, about 3 minutes. Beat in eggs, one at a time, beating well after each addition. Add flour mixture; beat on low until well mixed.

2. Roll dough into 1½-inch balls. Place on lightly greased baking sheet; bake until set but not browned, 8 to 10 minutes. Cool completely on wire rack.

3. Whisk together confectioners' sugar and milk in medium bowl until smooth. Divide glaze into small bowls and tint to desired colors using food coloring. Dip tops of cookies into glaze. Allow to dry on wire rack.

Butter Cookies You'd Eat in a Dream

This recipe came from Agnes Da Costa, who received an honorable mention in the 1989 contest. The dough needs no chilling, rolling or cutting, and it is easily doubled.

1	cup (2 sticks) butter, softened
½	cup plus 1½ tablespoons sugar
1¾	cups all-purpose flour
1	teaspoon vanilla
	Sugar for rolling

Prep time: 15 minutes

Bake time: 17 to 20 minutes per batch

1. Heat oven to 300 degrees. Cream butter and sugar. Add flour, a little at a time, then vanilla. Stir until blended.

2. Roll dough into small balls the size of a walnut, then roll the balls in sugar. Flatten with cookie stamp or bottom of a glass. Put onto ungreased cookie sheet. Bake until edges are lightly browned, 17 to 20 minutes.

Sugar
&
Spice

SUGAR & SPICE

Yield: About 8 dozen cookies

Pictured on p. 74

Christmas Ginger Cookies

These ginger cookies, flavored with an abundance of fresh orange rind, captured third place for Janis C. Peterson in 1991. The rolled, cutout cookies are easy to bake and have a delicious combination of fresh tastes.

Dough:

1	cup (2 sticks) unsalted butter or margarine, softened
1¼	cups granulated sugar
1	large egg
2	tablespoons dark corn syrup
1½	tablespoons grated orange rind
1	tablespoon water
3¼	cups all-purpose flour
2	teaspoons baking soda
2	teaspoons cinnamon
1	teaspoon ginger
½	teaspoon cloves
¼	teaspoon salt

Icing:

1	large egg white
1	teaspoon almond extract
2–4	cups confectioners' sugar, as needed

Prep time: 30 minutes

Chill time: Overnight

Bake time: 8 to 10 minutes per batch

1. Cream butter and sugar in large mixer bowl with electric mixer. Beat in egg until light. Stir in corn syrup, orange rind and water. Mix flour, baking soda, cinnamon, ginger, cloves and salt. Stir into butter mixture to form a dough. Divide dough in half. Wrap in wax paper and refrigerate overnight.

2. Heat oven to 325 degrees. Have lightly greased baking sheets ready.

3. Roll out one piece of dough at a time on a lightly floured surface or between sheets of floured wax paper to ⅛-inch thickness. Cut into shapes with cookie cutters. Place on baking sheets, leaving 2 inches between each cookie. Bake until golden, 8 to 10 minutes. Transfer to wire racks to cool.

4. For icing, mix egg white and almond extract in small bowl until frothy. Stir in confectioners' sugar until mixture is a drizzling consistency. Drizzle over cookies. Let stand until icing sets. Store covered.

Note: This recipe uses raw egg white. Cases of salmonella poisoning have been traced to raw eggs, although this is rare and usually associated with the yolks.

Yield: About 30 cookies

Eggnog Cookies

Rich Ptack and his daughter Sarah created this recipe after years of baking together, and it earned them an honorable mention in 2013. The cookie has a warm nutmeg accent, and its flavor mimics the traditional holiday drink. These cookies bake at a lower temperature than most so that they do not dry out.

2¼	cups flour
1	teaspoon baking powder
1	teaspoon nutmeg, plus more for sprinkling
½	teaspoon cinnamon
1½	sticks (¾ cup) butter, softened
1¼	cup sugar
½	cup store-bought eggnog
2	egg yolks
1	teaspoon vanilla

Prep time: 20 minutes

Bake time: 20 to 23 minutes per batch

1. Heat the oven to 300 degrees. Combine the flour, baking powder, 1 teaspoon nutmeg and cinnamon in a bowl.

2. Cream the butter and sugar in a separate bowl with an electric mixer until light and fluffy. Add eggnog, egg yolks and vanilla. Beat on medium speed until smooth. Add flour mixture; beat at low speed until just combined. You don't want to overmix.

3. Scoop up dough by heaping spoonfuls; roll into balls. Place the balls onto parchment-lined cookie sheets 1 inch apart. Sprinkle lightly with nutmeg. Bake until bottoms turn light brown, 20 to 23 minutes.

Yield: 3 to 4 dozen large bears

Gingerbread Bears

When Nancy Schubert was growing up, "Gingerbread Saturday" was a tradition in her house, and she and her sister would spend the day rolling dough, cutting shapes, and baking and decorating cookies. To bedeck these chubby little bears – a recipe that took first place in 1992 – she used colored sugar, little candies and a classic royal icing. Confectioners' sugar icing or tubes of decorator icing can also be used.

3½ cups unsifted all-purpose flour

1½ teaspoons ginger

1½ teaspoons cinnamon

1 teaspoon cloves

1 teaspoon baking soda

¼ teaspoon salt

½ cup (1 stick) butter, softened

¾ cup sugar

1 large egg

¾ cup light molasses

1 teaspoon grated lemon rind

Decorations as desired

Prep time: 35 minutes

Chill time: 2 hours or overnight

Bake time: 7 to 10 minutes per batch

1. Measure 3½ cups flour; sift together with spices, baking soda and salt; set aside. Beat butter with an electric mixer in a large bowl until smooth. Add sugar and mix on high speed until light and fluffy, 2 minutes. Add egg and mix well. Stop the mixer and add molasses and lemon rind. Mix on low speed to combine. Stir in dry ingredients with a wooden spoon.

2. Divide dough into four parts. Wrap each one separately in plastic wrap and refrigerate 2 hours or overnight.

3. Heat oven to 375 degrees. Lightly grease baking sheets.

4. Remove one piece of dough from the refrigerator at a time. Roll the well-chilled dough on a floured board or between sheets of wax paper to ⅛-inch thickness. Cut out with cookie cutters and carefully transfer to prepared baking sheets, leaving 1 inch between each cookie.

5. Bake just until the cookies are lightly browned and set, 7 to 10 minutes. Do not overbake. Transfer from baking sheets to a wire rack and cool completely before decorating. Decorate as desired. Store in airtight containers.

Yield: About 4 dozen cookies

Pictured on p. 56

Mom's Sugar Cookies

Nancy Rullo's beautiful Santa Claus cutout cookies are made from a basic dough and a cream-cheese frosting. Rullo wrote that as children, she and her brother used to help cut out the Santa Claus shapes and watch them bake. She won second place for the nostalgic recipe in 1990.

Dough:

1	cup (2 sticks) unsalted butter, softened
1½	cups confectioners' sugar
1	large egg
1	teaspoon vanilla
½	teaspoon almond extract
2½	cups flour
1	teaspoon baking soda
1	teaspoon cream of tartar

Frosting:

1	package (8 ounces) cream cheese, softened
2	cups confectioners' sugar
¼	teaspoon vanilla
	Milk
	Food coloring as desired

Prep time: 30 minutes

Chill time: 2 to 3 hours

Bake time: 7 to 8 minutes per batch

1. Cream butter, sugar, egg, vanilla and almond extract in large mixer bowl until light and fluffy. Beat in flour, baking soda and cream of tartar until mixed. Divide dough in half. Cover and refrigerate dough 2 to 3 hours. (Dough can be refrigerated up to several days; soften slightly before rolling out.)

2. Heat oven to 350 degrees. Have lightly greased baking sheets ready.

3. Roll out half of dough on lightly floured surface to almost ¼-inch thickness. Use cookie cutters to cut out desired shapes. Place cookies 2 inches apart on prepared baking sheets. Bake until light brown on edges, 7 to 8 minutes. Cool on wire racks.

4. For frosting, beat cream cheese, sugar and vanilla in small bowl until smooth. Beat in milk until spreading consistency. Add food coloring as desired.

5. Use frosting to decorate cookies. Let stand until frosting sets.

Yield: 6 dozen cookies

Pat Egan's Christmas Tree Cookies

Pat Egan made this recipe with her 4-year-old daughter, winning second place in 1988. The cookies are easily shaped into Christmas trees and edged with glittery green sugar.

2½ cups flour

1 cup sugar

1 cup (2 sticks) butter or margarine, softened

1½ teaspoons baking powder

¼ teaspoon salt

½ teaspoon almond extract

1 large egg

¼ cup green sugar crystals, about

¼ cup confetti or nonpareil candy decorations, optional

Prep time: 20 minutes

Chill time: 4 hours

Bake time: 10 minutes per batch

1. Put flour, sugar, butter, baking powder, salt, almond extract and egg into large bowl of an electric mixer. Mix together, using low speed. Dough will be crumbly. Knead dough with hands until mixture holds together.

2. Remove ⅓ cup of the dough; wrap and refrigerate. Divide remaining dough in thirds. Using hands, roll each into a 6-inch log.

3. Put sugar crystals on a sheet of wax paper. Roll each log in the sugar crystals to coat well; use the wax paper as a guide to press in crystals. Shape each log into a triangle, pressing gently on wax paper to give 3 sharp corners. Make sure to make 2 sides longer than the third side. Wrap each log well and refrigerate at least 4 hours or until dough is firm enough to slice. To this point, cookies can be made up to a week in advance.

4. Heat oven to 350 degrees. To bake, slice logs cross-wise into ¼-inch slices. Put slices about 1 inch apart on ungreased cookie sheets. For each cookie, shape about ½ teaspoon of the reserved ⅓ cup dough into a tree trunk. Attach to bottom underside of each tree. Sprinkle each cookie lightly with candy decorations, if desired. Bake until lightly browned, about 10 minutes. Carefully remove to wire racks. Cool completely.

Note: The logs can be divided and shaped into 3 sizes and sliced to form a 3-tiered tree.

Note: After the 12-hour resting period, this cookie dough can be hand-molded like clay — rolled, pinched, poked and pressed — and it will keep its shape, expanding slightly while baking. Thin cookies will become brown and bake quickly; large and thick shapes will require longer baking.

Yield: About 80 2½-inch cookies

1 cup granulated sugar
½ cup dark corn syrup
½ cup water
1 tablespoon ginger
2 teaspoons cinnamon
2 teaspoons cloves
1 cup (2 sticks) unsalted butter or margarine
4 cups all-purpose flour
1½ teaspoons baking soda
Liquid food coloring, if desired

Prep time: 1½ hours

Chill time: 12 hours or more

Bake time: 7 minutes per batch

Ginger Cookies

Judith Taylor said this cookie recipe, which won first place in 1993, allowed her to combine her love for both art and ginger because the dough can be cut into any shape desired and used to make decorations. "People often tell me the cookies are too pretty to eat," Taylor said. "But the cookies are definitely meant to be eaten." She also advised making the cookies uniformly thick and said a microwave can be used to cook the sugar mixture in step 1.

1. Put sugar, syrup, water, ginger, cinnamon and cloves into a large saucepan. Cook and stir over medium heat until mixture boils and sugar dissolves. Remove from heat. Add butter. Stir until butter is melted and mixture is no longer very hot.

2. Mix flour and baking soda. Gradually add flour mixture to butter mixture and stir to blend thoroughly. Dough will have a soft texture. Place dough in an airtight container and refrigerate overnight or at least 12 hours or as long as 1 week.

3. Heat oven to 375 degrees. Remove about ⅙ of the dough and knead it until it is slightly softened. Roll dough directly onto ungreased cookie sheets until it is about ¼ inch thick. Use a cookie cutter to stamp shapes in dough, allowing a 1-inch margin between each cookie. Remove excess dough by lifting it and peeling it away. Scraps of dough can be kneaded together and re-rolled.

4. Bake until golden brown, about 7 minutes. Allow cookies to cool slightly and become crisp before removing them from the cookie sheet. Cool thoroughly on wire racks. If desired, you may "paint" the cooled cookies using a clean, small paintbrush and food coloring that has been watered down slightly. Store cookies in airtight containers.

Shortbread Cookies

Yield: About 4 dozen cookies

This simple shortbread cookie recipe from Sandra Petrille uses brown sugar instead of white. Petrille, who won second prize for these cookies in 1996, said the recipe is so easy, she hesitated to enter it.

4 cups all-purpose flour

1 cup packed light brown sugar

1 pound (4 sticks) unsalted butter, softened

Prep time: 25 minutes

Bake time: 8 to 10 minutes per batch

1. Heat oven to 325 degrees. Beat all ingredients in large bowl of electric mixer on medium-high speed until smooth, about 4 minutes.

2. Divide dough into 4 pieces. Roll out 1 piece of dough at a time on lightly floured surface to $\frac{1}{16}$- to $\frac{1}{8}$-inch thickness. Cut out dough with cookie cutters.

3. Bake cookies on ungreased baking sheet until pale brown and slightly firm to the touch, 8 to 10 minutes. Remove to cooling rack. Decorate as desired.

Mutti's Butter Cookies

Ivy Risch's recipe, which scored the No. 2 spot in 2009, traces back to her missionary grandparents' years in China and her grandmother's friendship with Madame Chiang Kai-shek. Her grandmother called the cookies "speculatius."

2½ sticks (1¼ cups) unsalted butter, softened

3 eggs

2 cups sugar

1 teaspoon salt

3 cups flour

¼ teaspoon cinnamon

Prep time: 75 minutes

Chill time: 1 hour

Bake time: 7 to 8 minutes per batch

1. Combine butter, eggs, sugar and salt in large bowl; stir with wooden spoon until smooth, about 1 minute. Combine 2¼ cups of the flour and cinnamon in a medium bowl; add to butter mixture 1 cup at a time, stirring to make a soft, sticky dough. Sprinkle remaining ¾ cup of the flour on counter; place dough on the flour. Knead, incorporating more flour just until dough is no longer sticky. Wrap dough in plastic wrap; refrigerate 1 hour or overnight.

2. Heat oven to 350 degrees. Remove dough from refrigerator; cut off a 2-inch piece. Re-wrap remaining dough; return to refrigerator. Roll dough out on a lightly floured surface to ⅛ inch thick. Cut shapes with cookie cutters. Transfer cookies to parchment-lined baking sheets; bake until edges turn golden brown, 7 to 8 minutes per batch. Transfer cookies to wire rack to cool. Repeat with remaining chilled dough.

Yield: 30 cookies
(depending on size)

Dough:

3 cups all-purpose flour

3 cups bread flour

2 teaspoons baking powder

1 pound unsalted butter, softened

1 cup granulated sugar

1 cup packed brown sugar

1 teaspoon salt

1 tablespoon vanilla

1 tablespoon 2% milk

3 large eggs plus 1 egg yolk

Royal Icing:

¼ cup meringue powder

1 pound powdered sugar
  Water, about ⅓ cup
  Gel food coloring

Prep time: 40 minutes, plus decorating

Chill time: 4 hours

Bake time: 12 to 15 minutes per batch

Snowflake Sugar Cookies

Meagan Fricano received an honorable mention in 2011 for these beautiful cookies, which shimmered, sparkled and glowed. Fricano, a neurobiologist, used forceps to apply her silver dragees.

1. Combine the flours and baking powder in a bowl; stir to evenly distribute the baking powder. Set aside.

2. In a 6-quart stand mixer with a paddle attachment, cream the butter and sugars until light and fluffy. Add the salt, vanilla and milk; mix to blend. With mixer running, add eggs and extra yolk, one at a time, waiting until each is combined before adding the next.

3. Reduce the mixer speed to low; slowly add flour mixture. Add additional all-purpose flour 1 tablespoon at a time until the dough is no longer sticky to the touch. Turn dough out onto plastic wrap; divide in half. Wrap each portion in plastic wrap; form into flat discs. Refrigerate 4 to 48 hours, or freeze up to a month.

4. Heat oven to 375 degrees. Let dough warm up slightly; roll out to ½ inch thick using powdered sugar (not flour) to stop it from sticking. Cut out snowflake shapes; bake on parchment-lined baking pans until just barely starting to brown on the edges, 12 to 15 minutes. Remove promptly from oven; let cool on the sheet pan, 2 minutes. Transfer to a wire rack to cool completely before decorating.

5. For icing, mix the meringue powder and powdered sugar in a medium bowl; slowly add water until the frosting reaches desired consistency. Add a little gel food coloring, if desired. For best results, start with a stiff frosting, put some aside in a parchment baking bag or zip-top bag, then add water to the remaining frosting. Use the stiff frosting to pipe outlines on the cooled cookies, then carefully apply the thinner icing to fill in the cookies between the piped outlines (a toothpick helps to carefully move thin icing into small spaces).

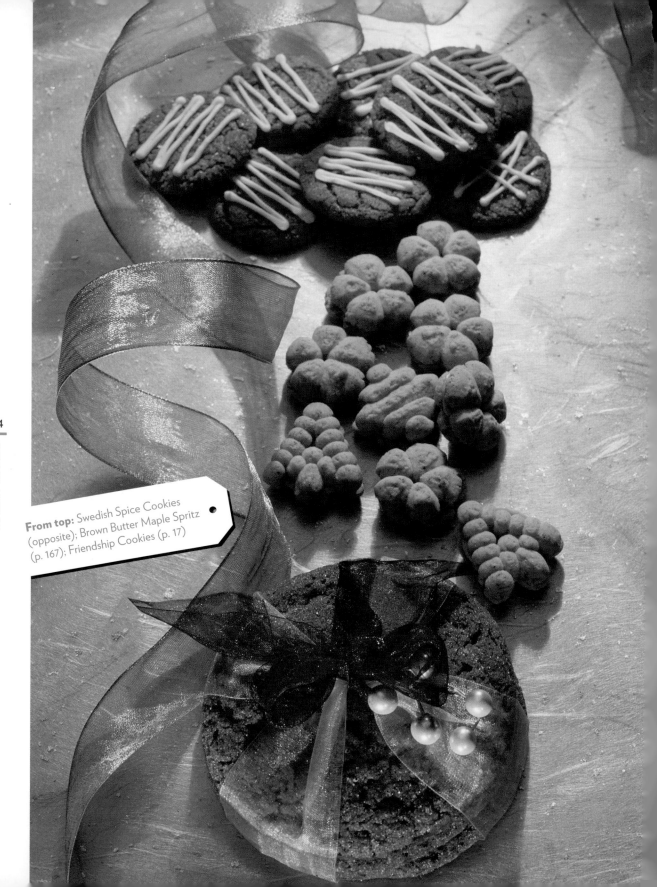

From top: Swedish Spice Cookies (opposite); Brown Butter Maple Spritz (p. 167); Friendship Cookies (p. 17)

Yield: About 5 dozen cookies

Swedish Spice Cookies

Colleen Ries' delightfully chewy and delicious cookies topped more than 325 entries in 1995 to win her the grand prize. Ries said she learned to bake alongside her grandmother, who used to save her seven cookies and write one letter of her name on each. These cookies can be left plain or be decorated or glazed as desired.

2¼ cups all-purpose flour, sifted before measuring

2 teaspoons baking soda

1 teaspoon cloves

1 teaspoon ginger

1 teaspoon cinnamon

1 teaspoon salt

¾ cup (1½ sticks) unsalted butter, softened

1½ cups sugar

1 large egg

¼ cup molasses

Prep time: 45 minutes

Bake time: 9 to 10 minutes per batch

1. Heat oven to 375 degrees. Have ungreased baking sheet(s) ready. Sift together the flour, baking soda, spices and salt; set aside.

2. Beat the butter and 1 cup of the granulated sugar in large bowl of an electric mixer on high speed until light, 1 minute. Add the egg and molasses; mix well. Stop the mixer and add the flour mixture. Mix just until combined.

3. Using about 1½ teaspoons dough for each, roll dough into balls. Roll in the remaining ½ cup granulated sugar so they are fully coated. Arrange on baking sheet, spacing them 2 inches apart. If you prefer a thin, crisp cookie, they may be flattened with a glass that has been dipped in sugar.

4. Bake until set, 9 to 10 minutes. Transfer to a wire rack and let cool.

Francine Palma Long wrote that as an internist, she liked this recipe for its oat and whole wheat flours and its "prudent calorie and fat content." She also said the spices and texture remind her of gingerbread, a Christmas favorite. The recipe received an honorable mention in 2013.

Yield: 5 dozen cookies

Ginger Spice Delights

Dough:

1½	cups rolled oats
5	tablespoons butter
⅓	cup granulated sugar
⅓	cup packed brown sugar
2	tablespoons freshly grated orange zest
½	cup light or dark molasses
7	tablespoons unsweetened applesauce
1	large egg yolk
1	teaspoon vanilla extract
1	teaspoon baking soda
1½	teaspoons cinnamon
1½	teaspoons ginger
½	teaspoon cloves
¼	teaspoon allspice
¼	teaspoon black pepper
¼	teaspoon salt
2¼	cups whole wheat flour

Sugar coating:

1	cup granulated sugar
2	tablespoons freshly grated orange zest

Prep time: 30 minutes

Bake time: 10 minutes per batch

1. Heat oven to 375 degrees. For the dough, grind the oats in a food processor until it looks like fine powder, 1 to 2 minutes.

2. Beat the butter and ⅓ cup granulated sugar in a large bowl with an electric mixer on medium-high speed until light and fluffy. Add the brown sugar and orange zest, continuing to beat as you add the molasses, applesauce, egg yolk and vanilla. Mix the baking soda, cinnamon, ginger, cloves, allspice, pepper and salt together in a bowl. Add to the dough. Beat on medium-high until well mixed.

3. Turn the mixer to medium; slowly add the ground oats. Then slowly add the whole wheat flour. The dough will be moderately sticky.

4. For the coating, pulse the sugar and orange zest in a food processor until well combined. Place in a shallow bowl.

5. Using a rounded teaspoon of dough per cookie, roll the dough into balls; roll each ball in the coating sugar. (If necessary, moisten your palms to help with rolling.) Place the balls about 1½ inches apart on parchment-lined cookie sheets.

6. Bake in batches until the edges are set and tops are cracked but the centers are still soft and puffy, about 10 minutes. Let the cookies cool on the baking sheets.

Linzer Perec

This delicate butter cookie earned Helen Salata an honorable mention in the 2004 contest. Salata's mother created the recipe through trial and error after arriving in the U.S. as a young and inexperienced cook.

2½ cups flour

½ teaspoon baking soda

2 sticks (1 cup) unsalted butter, room temperature

½ cup sugar

2 egg yolks

Zest of ½ lemon

¼ cup milk

1 egg white, beaten

¼ cup apricot preserves or preserve flavor of choice

Prep time: 1 hour

Chill time: 30 minutes

Bake time: 8 minutes per batch

1. Sift together flour and baking soda; set aside. Beat butter with a mixer on medium-high speed until smooth. Add sugar, egg yolks and lemon zest, beating until creamy. Add flour mixture and milk, alternating gradually until the dough comes together and becomes smooth but not hard, with no ingredients sticking to the sides or bottom of bowl.

2. Pat the dough into 3 rounds. Cover with plastic wrap. Refrigerate at least 30 minutes.

3. Heat oven to 375 degrees. Roll out the first round to about ⅜ inch thick. Cut into circles with 1½-inch cookie cutter. Make a ¾-inch hole in the center of half of the rounds with a thimble or non-piping end of a pastry tip. Brush tops (the pieces with holes) with egg white; lightly dip in sugar. Place tops and bottoms on an ungreased cookie sheet. Bake until beginning to brown around the edges, about 8 minutes. Cool on wire rack. Repeat with remaining dough.

4. To assemble, spread preserves lightly on cookie bottoms; cover with tops, pressing gently to avoid cracking.

Yield: 64 cookies

Sweet and Savory Shortbread Cookies

1 cup flour

1 teaspoon baking soda

1 teaspoon cream of tartar

1 stick (½ cup) butter, room temperature

½ cup confectioners' sugar

¼ cup granulated sugar

½ teaspoon vanilla

1 cup chocolate-covered raisins, finely chopped

1 tablespoon light corn syrup

¾ cup finely crushed butter-flavored pretzels

Prep time: 30 minutes

Chill time: 1 hour

Bake time: 10 minutes per batch

1. Sift together flour, baking soda and cream of tartar in a medium bowl; set aside.

2. Combine butter and sugars in a large bowl; beat with a mixer on medium speed until light and fluffy. Add vanilla; beat until fluffy, about 2 minutes. Reduce speed to low; beat flour mixture into butter mixture in batches, until just mixed. Stir in raisins.

3. Shape dough into 2 logs, about 8-by-1-inch each. Brush logs all over with corn syrup. Place pretzel crumbs on a plate; roll logs in pretzel crumbs. Return logs to plate; loosely cover with plastic wrap. Refrigerate until firm, about 1 hour.

4. Heat oven to 350 degrees. Cut dough into ¼-inch slices; transfer to a lightly greased baking sheet. Bake until slightly brown around the edges, about 10 minutes. Transfer cookies to a wire rack to cool.

Jelly Thumbprints (p. 108)

Nancy Vaziri created this recipe **without eggs or nuts** to accommodate her grandson's allergies. The 2005 third-place winner also incorporates some of his favorite snack foods, which account for its pebbly texture and crunchy edges. These cookies live up to their name with their zesty blend of flavors, including salty crushed pretzels and sweet chewy raisins.

Yield: 5 dozen cookies

Pictured on p. 112

Sirapskakor (Syrup Cookies)

The dough in this recipe might require a bit of kneading to come together for this tender, crisp cookie. Created by Jo Anne Lightfoot, it won first prize winner in the 2004 contest. Because these cookies don't spread when baking, they can be placed closely together on the baking sheet. You can decorate these cookies with an optional glaze or use holiday cookie cutters if you prefer more festive shapes.

Dough:

2½ cups flour

2 teaspoons baking soda

1 cup granulated sugar

1 stick (½ cup) plus 6 tablespoons unsalted butter, cut into tablespoons

2 teaspoons molasses

Glaze (optional):

½ cup confectioners' sugar

2¼ teaspoons prepared coffee

Prep time: 25 minutes

Bake time: 10 minutes per batch

1. Heat oven to 350 degrees. Sift together flour and baking soda; set aside. Beat sugar, butter and molasses with a mixer on medium-high speed. Slowly add dry ingredients until just mixed.

2. Roll dough ⅛ inch thick on lightly floured surface. Cut into parallelogram strips (see picture), 1¼ by 3½ inches, and place on lightly greased baking sheet. Bake until lightly brown, about 10 minutes. Cool on rack.

3. Meanwhile, for glaze, whisk together sugar and coffee until smooth. Ice cookies lightly with a knife, or fill a small pastry bag with glaze. Drizzle over cookies.

Gloria Heeter's Best Gingerbread Cookies

Gloria Heeter described these spicy gingerbread cookies as being "for all seasons." She got the recipe from a neighbor who once brought over a batch for Halloween. At Christmas, Heeter cuts them into gingerbread people, writes names on them, and hands them out as gifts. The multi-purpose cookies won third place in 1988.

Dough:

1 cup (2 sticks) corn oil margarine

1 cup sugar

1 cup molasses

1 large egg

4 cups flour

2 teaspoons baking powder

1 teaspoon baking soda

3 teaspoons cinnamon

2 teaspoons cloves

2 teaspoons ginger

1 teaspoon nutmeg

   Currants, raisins, silver balls and candy for decoration

1 large egg yolk mixed with 1 teaspoon water

Icing:

Confectioners' sugar

Water

Food coloring

Prep time: 25 minutes

Chill time: 8 hours or overnight

Bake time: 7 to 10 minutes per batch

1. Beat margarine, sugar and molasses in a large mixing bowl. Add egg and mix well.

2. Sift together flour, baking powder, baking soda, cinnamon, cloves, ginger and nutmeg. Add to butter mixture; mix well.

3. Divide dough into 4 equal portions on a large piece of plastic wrap. Wrap and shape into a flat disc about 1 inch thick. Refrigerate until firm, about 8 hours, or freeze for 2 hours. (Dough can be refrigerated up to 3 days.)

4. Heat oven to 350 degrees. Working with 1 disc of the dough at a time, roll out on a well-floured board, dusting the rolling pin as you work. Dough will be very soft and can be difficult to work with so work quickly and use plenty of flour. Using cookie cutters dipped in flour, cut into desired shapes. Put cookies 1 inch apart on an ungreased cookie sheet. Use currants or candy for eyes or buttons, if desired.

5. Bake until lightly puffed, 7 to 10 minutes. First batch may be puffier because they will have less flour rolled in them. While still warm, paint with egg yolk wash if desired. Cool on wire racks. Cool completely, then decorate as desired with icing.

6. For icing, mix confectioners' sugar with a small amount of water until thick and of spreading consistency. Add food coloring if desired and put in a small plastic bag. Cut a small hole in one corner and drizzle icing out onto the cooled cookies.

Note: A 4-inch gingerbread cookie cutter was used in testing.

Sparkly Oatmeal Cookies

Andra Weber's oatmeal cookies owe their sparkle to decorative sugars. The recipe earned her a second place finish in the 2007 contest. For smaller cookies, make 1-inch dough balls and flatten them into 2-inch cookies.

Dough:

1½ cups flour

2 teaspoons baking powder

1 teaspoon cinnamon

1 teaspoon baking soda

1 teaspoon salt

¼ teaspoon freshly grated nutmeg

2½ sticks (1¼ cups) unsalted butter, softened

¾ cup packed light brown sugar

½ cup granulated sugar

1 egg

1 teaspoon vanilla

1¾ cups old-fashioned rolled oats, finely ground in blender or food processor

Frosting:

1 cup sifted confectioners' sugar

½ teaspoon vanilla

½ teaspoon almond extract

1 tablespoon milk

Decorative sugars

Prep time: 15 minutes

Bake time: 10 to 12 minutes per batch

1. Heat the oven to 375 degrees. Sift together the flour, baking powder, cinnamon, baking soda, salt and nutmeg; set aside. Beat together the butter and sugars with a mixer on medium speed in a large bowl until light and fluffy; beat in the egg and vanilla. Stir in the flour mixture and oats until well combined.

2. Arrange rounded 2-inch balls of dough about 3 inches apart on an ungreased baking sheet; flatten into 4-inch rounds about ½ inch thick with the bottom of a small floured juice glass. Bake cookies in batches until golden, about 10 to 12 minutes. Cool cookies on sheets 2 minutes; transfer to wire racks. Cool completely.

3. For frosting, mix all ingredients in a small bowl with a fork until smooth. Spread over cookies. Top with decorative sugars. Store in an airtight container.

From top: Nut Crescents (p. 96),
Shortbread Sheep (opposite),
Mom's Sugar Cookies (p. 36)

Shortbread Sheep

Betty J. Koenig used a sheep cookie cutter to make these cookies, which won third place in 1990. She suggested using your fingertips to dimple the dough to resemble their wooly coats. If desired, a small piece of chocolate can be used for eyes after baking.

2 cups (1 pound) unsalted butter, softened

1 cup sugar

4 cups flour

¼ teaspoon salt

Prep time: 25 minutes

Bake time: 20 to 25 minutes per batch

1. Cream butter and sugar in large mixer bowl until light and fluffy. Beat in flour and salt. Knead the dough briefly until smooth. If dough is too sticky, add a bit more flour. (Dough can be refrigerated up to several days; soften slightly before shaping cookies.)

2. Heat oven to 325 degrees. Have ungreased baking sheets ready.

3. Pat half of the dough out on lightly floured surface to ½-inch thickness. Use cookie cutters to cut out desired shapes. Place cookies 2 inches apart on baking sheets. Bake until light brown on edges, 20 to 25 minutes. Cool on wire racks.

Note: The sheep cookie cutter used by Koenig is a Hallmark cutter that is no longer available. A sheep pattern can be made out of cardboard and placed over dough; cut out the shape with a small knife.

Wanderer Cookies

Beth Petti created these spicy, glazed star cookies that won an honorable mention in the 2000 contest.

4 cups flour

1 teaspoon baking soda

1 teaspoon cloves

1 teaspoon nutmeg

1 teaspoon cinnamon

1 cup chopped candied fruit

1 cup chopped walnuts

2 sticks (1 cup) butter

2½ cups confectioners' sugar

3 eggs

1–2 tablespoons hot water

Prep time: 1 hour

Bake time: 20 minutes per batch

1. Heat oven to 300 degrees. Stir flour, baking soda, cloves, nutmeg and cinnamon together in medium bowl. Stir in fruit and walnuts until fruit is lightly coated and separated; set aside. Beat butter with 1½ cups of the sugar until light and fluffy. Beat in eggs one at a time. Mix in flour mixture until combined.

2. Roll out dough ¼ inch thick on lightly floured surface. Use sharp, 2-inch star-shape cutter to cut cookies. Place cookies on ungreased baking sheet. Bake until bottoms are golden, about 20 minutes. Cool slightly on wire rack.

3. Stir 1 tablespoon of the water, or more if needed, into remaining 1 cup sugar to make medium-thick, smooth glaze. Drizzle glaze over cookies in stripes while cookies are still warm.

Polvorones

You'll be licking your fingers after eating one of these sugar-dusted spice cookies from Nora Grindheim, who received an honorable mention in the 2001 contest.

Dough:

2   sticks (1 cup) unsalted butter

½   cup confectioners' sugar

2   tablespoons milk

1   teaspoon vanilla extract

½   teaspoon cinnamon

1½ cups flour

1   teaspoon baking powder

Sugar coating:

½   cup sugar

¼   teaspoon cinnamon

½   square (½ ounce) finely grated semisweet chocolate

Prep time: 15 minutes

Bake time: 20 minutes per batch

1. Heat oven to 325 degrees. Cream butter, sugar, milk, vanilla and cinnamon in the bowl of an electric mixer until light and fluffy, scraping down side of bowl once, 3 minutes. Sift together flour and baking powder; add gradually to the butter mixture.

2. Roll dough into ½-inch balls. Place 3 inches apart on greased cookie sheets. Flatten into 2-inch rounds with bottom of glass dipped in granulated sugar. Bake until edges are golden brown, about 20 minutes. Cool on cookie sheet, 3-4 minutes.

3. For sugar coating, combine sugar, cinnamon and chocolate in a low, flat container. Coat cookies on both sides with sugar mixture. Place on cooling racks. Cool completely.

The winning cookies of 1998, including Crescent Cookies (following page)

Crescent Cookies

A few years after her grandmother passed away, Anne Marie Reband unexpectedly found this recipe in her grandmother's file box. These delicate cookies won second place in the 1998 contest.

½ cup (1 stick) butter, softened

½ cup solid shortening

⅓ cup granulated sugar

⅔ cup finely chopped walnuts

1⅔ cups all-purpose flour

¼ teaspoon salt

1 cup confectioners' sugar, plus more for sprinkling

1 teaspoon cinnamon

Prep time: 35 minutes

Chill time: 2 hours or overnight

Bake time: 14 to 16 minutes per batch

1. Beat butter, shortening and granulated sugar in bowl of electric mixer until light and fluffy, about 3 minutes. Beat in nuts. Add flour and salt; beat on low until combined. Wrap dough in plastic wrap; refrigerate 2 hours or overnight.

2. Heat oven to 325 degrees. Roll dough into ½-inch-thick rope; cut into 2-inch lengths. Form dough into crescents; place on ungreased baking sheet. Bake until set but not browned, 14 to 16 minutes. Cool 5 minutes on sheet; remove to wire rack. Sift together confectioners' sugar and cinnamon. Dip cookies into mixture while still warm; cool completely. Sprinkle with additional confectioners' sugar before serving, if desired.

Iced Christmas Shortbread Cookies

Joyce Gephart's friend described these cookies as "sinfully delicate and crispy." Gephart's "sinful" recipe received an honorable mention in 1997.

Dough:

1 cup butter

½ cup sugar

½ teaspoon lemon extract

2½ cups flour

Icing:

½ cup butter

1¼ cups confectioners' sugar

1 teaspoon vanilla extract

1 teaspoon milk

Red, green food coloring

🕐 **Prep time:** 15 minutes

Chill time: 30 minutes

Bake time: 22 minutes per batch

1. Heat oven to 300 degrees. Beat butter with sugar in mixing bowl until fluffy. Add lemon extract. Stir in flour in 3 parts, beating well after each addition; dough will be stiff.

2. Knead in bowl 5 minutes, or until smooth. Wrap dough in wax paper and chill 30 minutes.

3. Roll teaspoon-size pieces of dough into balls and place 2 inches apart on ungreased cookies sheets. Flatten balls to ¼-inch thickness. Bake 22 minutes or until slightly colored.

4. For icing, melt ½ cup butter and add enough confectioners' sugar to achieve spreading consistency. Add vanilla and milk. Divide icing into 2 bowls. Tint 1 with red food coloring and the other with green. Spread on cooled cookies.

Yield: About 3 dozen cookies

Mexican Mice

Caryn Lerner created these "mice" because her nieces and nephews wouldn't eat her traditional Mexican wedding cake cookies. She decorated the cookies with almond ears, chocolate whiskers, and chow-mein-noodle tails, winning second place in the 2000 contest.

2   sticks (1 cup) butter, softened

1   teaspoon vanilla extract

½   cup confectioners' sugar, plus more for dusting

2   cups flour

1   cup finely ground pecans

¼   teaspoon salt

Chow mein noodles

Mini-chocolate chips

Sliced almonds

Prep time: 1 hour

Bake time: 27 minutes per batch

1. Heat oven to 350 degrees. Beat butter and vanilla in bowl of electric mixer until light and fluffy. Add sugar; beat until combined. Mix in flour, pecans and salt.

2. Shape dough into 1-inch ovals, tapering one end. Bake 15 minutes. Remove from oven; insert noodle at tail end and 2 almonds about ⅓ of the way from pointed end for ears. Return to oven; bake until slightly browned, about 12 minutes.

3. Remove from oven; immediately place 2 chocolate chips in front of ears for eyes. (Chocolate will melt slightly and stick to cookie.) Dust mice bodies with confectioners' sugar. Cool on wire rack.

Yield: 3 dozen cookies

Orange Pecan Ice Box Cookies

Marie Carlson's delicate, old-fashioned cookies add a graceful touch to dessert trays. Carlson, an honorable mention recipient in the 2002 contest, said she remembers her mother greeting her with these orange pecan bars after school in the 1940s.

2	sticks (1 cup) butter
½	cup granulated sugar
½	cup light brown sugar
1	egg
2	tablespoons orange juice
1	tablespoon orange zest
2¾	cups flour
1	teaspoon baking soda
½	cup chopped pecans

Prep time: 30 minutes

Chill time: 8 hours

Bake time: 10 minutes per batch

1. Beat butter and granulated sugar in bowl of electric mixer until light, about 3 minutes. Beat in brown sugar, egg, orange juice and zest on medium speed; stir in flour and baking soda. Stir in nuts; shape into two 9-by-2½-inch bars; wrap in plastic wrap. Chill 8 hours.

2. Heat oven to 350 degrees; cut bars into thin slices. Place on lightly greased baking sheets; bake until edges begin to brown, about 10 minutes. Cool on wire racks.

Yield: 3 dozen 5-inch cookies

Great-Grandma's Gingerbread Cookies

This 1989 second-place winner from Ann Smith came all the way from Bohemia, where Smith's great-grandmother lived before moving to the U.S. in 1872. Relocating to a small Czech-American town in South Dakota, she used to give her neighbors Old World gingerbread men, reindeer, and rocking horses at Christmas. The recipe includes sorghum, which gives the cookies a special flavor, but molasses can be used as a substitute.

½ cup solid vegetable shortening

1 cup sugar

3 large eggs

½ cup cold water

2 teaspoons baking soda

1 cup sorghum or molasses

5-6 cups all-purpose flour

1 teaspoon cinnamon

1 teaspoon ginger

½ teaspoon cloves

½ teaspoon salt

Prep time: 30 minutes

Chill time: Overnight

Bake time: 10 to 12 minutes per batch

1. Cream shortening and sugar in mixing bowl, beat in eggs, one at a time. Mix water and baking soda in small bowl until dissolved. Add baking soda mixture and sorghum to butter mixture. Sift 5½ cups of the flour, the spices and salt together. Blend into dough. Divide dough into 4 balls. Wrap in plastic wrap. Flatten and refrigerate overnight.

2. Heat oven to 350 degrees. Roll 1 portion of dough out at a time on lightly floured surface. Cut into desired shapes. Bake on a greased cookie sheet until puffed, 10 to 12 minutes. Do not overbake.

3. When cool, decorate with buttercream frosting and/or candies as desired.

From top: Melt Aways (p. 87); Cinnamon Toffee Bars (p. 192); Great-Grandma's Gingerbread Cookies (opposite)

Pumpkin Maple Dreams

Holly L. Sheridan received an honorable mention in the 2000 contest for these rich, nutty cookies.

Dough:

2½   cups flour

2   teaspoons pumpkin pie spice

1   teaspoon baking powder

1   teaspoon baking soda

1½   teaspoons salt

2   sticks (1 cup) butter

¼   cup shortening

1½   cups sugar

1   egg

1   can (15 ounces) pumpkin purée

1   teaspoon vanilla extract

1   cup raisins

Maple frosting:

3   tablespoons butter, softened

1½   cups confectioners' sugar

1½   tablespoons milk

¾   teaspoon maple flavoring

¼   teaspoon vanilla extract

½   cup chopped nuts, such as pecans or walnuts

Prep time:
1 hour, 15 minutes

Bake time: 15 minutes per batch

1. Heat oven to 350 degrees. Combine flour, pumpkin pie spice, baking powder, baking soda and salt in bowl; set aside. Beat butter, shortening and sugar in bowl of electric mixer until light and fluffy. Add egg; mix well. Add pumpkin and vanilla; mix until incorporated. Slowly mix in flour mixture until combined. Stir in raisins. Drop by tablespoon onto greased baking sheet. Bake until set, about 15 minutes. Cool on wire racks.

2. For frosting, cream butter in bowl of electric mixer. Gradually add sugar, alternating with milk, beating well after each addition, until smooth and fluffy. Mix in maple flavoring and vanilla. Spread (or pipe with star-tipped pastry bag) a thin layer of frosting on top of each cookie. Sprinkle with nuts.

FRUIT
& NUT
TREATS

FRUIT & NUT TREATS

Yield: 2 dozen cookies

Fay Kuhn's Thumbprints

This delightful buttery cookie crumbles as it melts in your mouth. Fay Kuhn said her family never had the time or money to bake Christmas cookies while she was growing up, but her mother started baking them when she retired. This recipe came from her mother's neighbor and won the 1988 contest.

½ cup (1 stick) butter

¼ cup sugar

½ teaspoon vanilla

1 large egg, separated

1 cup flour

¼ teaspoon salt

1¼ cups finely chopped nuts

¼ cup raspberry jam

Prep time: 20 minutes

Chill time: 1 hour

Bake time: 15 to 18 minutes per batch

1. Beat together butter and sugar in a mixer bowl. Add vanilla and egg yolk. Mix well.

2. Mix flour and salt, add to butter mixture and mix well. Cover; refrigerate at least 1 hour.

3. Heat oven to 325 degrees. Shape dough into 1-inch balls. Beat egg white lightly in a small bowl. Put nuts in another small bowl. Dip each ball into egg white, then roll in nuts. Put balls 1 inch apart on ungreased cookie sheet. Press thumb in the center of each to make an indentation.

4. Bake until light golden, 15 to 18 minutes. Cool on wire racks. Fill indentation with a small amount of raspberry jam.

Yield: About 4 dozen
cookies

Bess' Christmas Kourambiethes (Greek Almond Shortbread Cookies)

Bess Gallanis Hayes received an honorable mention in the 1996 contest for these Greek almond shortbread cookies.

½ cup blanched almonds

1 pound (4 sticks) unsalted butter, softened

1 box (1 pound) confectioners' sugar

2 egg yolks

3 tablespoons Cognac

1 teaspoon vanilla extract

3 cups cake flour

½ teaspoon baking powder

Prep time: 30 minutes

Bake time: 15 minutes per batch

1. Heat oven to 350 degrees. Spread almonds in a single layer on baking sheet. Bake, stirring occasionally, until lightly toasted, about 10 minutes. Remove from oven; cool, then chop coarsely.

2. Beat butter in large bowl of electric mixer on medium-high speed until very light and fluffy, 5 minutes. Add 3 tablespoons of the confectioners' sugar; continue beating 3 minutes.

3. Add egg yolks, Cognac and vanilla; beat until smooth. Beat in almonds, flour and baking powder until mixed well. (If dough is too soft to handle, add additional flour.)

4. Shape scant tablespoons full of dough between palms into round balls or crescents. Bake on ungreased baking sheet until set and very pale golden in color, 15 minutes. Remove cookies to cooling rack.

5. Place remaining confectioners' sugar into sifter. While cookies are still hot, sift confectioners' sugar over tops. Repeat twice at 20-minute intervals.

From top left: Christmas Ginger Cookies (p. 31); Oma's Almond Cookies (p. 97); Caramel Pecan Treasures (p. 82)

Christmas Rocks

The recipe for Phyllis Theodos' soft, fruit-studded morsels, which won third place in 1995, comes from her grandmother, who used to hand it out to valued customers of the Hollywood diner she owned in the 1940s.

3	cups all-purpose flour
1	tablespoon unsweetened cocoa
¾	teaspoon baking soda
1	teaspoon cinnamon
1	teaspoon mace
1	teaspoon nutmeg
½	teaspoon ginger
½	teaspoon allspice
¼	pound candied pineapple
¼	pound citron
¼	pound candied orange peel
¼	pound pitted dates
¼	pound figs
¼	cup dried or candied cherries
1	pound chopped pecans
1	cup raisins
½	cup dried currants
1	cup (2 sticks) unsalted butter, softened
1½	cups sugar
3	large eggs
1	tablespoon cold, strong coffee

1. Heat oven to 350 degrees. Have ready ungreased or parchment-lined baking sheet(s). Sift together the flour, cocoa, baking soda and spices. Cut candied fruits, dates and figs into small pieces and toss with a small amount of the flour mixture. Combine in a large bowl with the pecans, raisins and currants. Set aside.

2. Beat butter and sugar in large bowl of electric mixer on high speed until light, about 2 minutes. Add the eggs, 1 at a time, mixing well after each addition. Mix in the coffee. Stop the mixer and add the flour mixture. Mix on low speed just until combined. Using a wooden spoon, fold in the fruit and nut mixture to coat all the pieces.

3. Drop batter onto baking sheet in walnut-size mounds leaving about 2 inches between each cookie. Bake until set and tops are lightly browned, 14 to 16 minutes. Transfer to a wire rack to cool. Store in an airtight container with a small wedge of apple to keep them soft. The cookies may be glazed or sprinkled with confectioners' sugar, if desired.

Prep time: 1 hour

Bake time: 14 to 16 minutes per batch

Maureen Yamashiro received an honorable mention for these jazzy little jewels in 2011. She said she came up with the recipe herself by **"focusing on the poor berry long relegated to a Thanksgiving side dish."**

Yield: 4 dozen tartlets

Cranberry-Cheesecake-Chocolate Tartlets

Pastry:

3 ounces cream cheese, room temperature

¼ pound unsalted butter, room temperature

¼ pound stick margarine, room temperature

¼ cup confectioners' sugar

2 cups flour

Cranberry relish:

1 bag (12 ounces) fresh cranberries

1 cup fresh orange juice from 3 large oranges

 Grated zest of 2 oranges

¼ cup agave syrup

½ cup sugar

1 cinnamon stick

 Pinch kosher salt

Cheesecake filling:

5 ounces cream cheese, room temperature

3 tablespoons sugar

1 egg

1 teaspoon vanilla

48 dark chocolate Hershey's Kisses

3 ounces white chocolate

Prep time: 60 minutes

Chill time: 1 hour

Bake time: 15 to 18 minutes per batch

1. For the pastry, cream the cream cheese, butter and margarine together with an electric mixer in a bowl; mix in confectioners' sugar. Mix in flour. Once fully incorporated, roll into a disc; wrap in plastic. Refrigerate at least 1 hour.

2. For the relish, combine cranberries, orange juice, zest, agave syrup, sugar, cinnamon stick and salt in a saucepan. Heat to a boil over medium heat; reduce to a steady simmer. Simmer until reduced to consistency of a good preserve, 30 minutes. Remove cinnamon stick.

3. For the filling, cream the cream cheese and sugar with an electric mixer in a bowl; add egg and vanilla. Mix until blended. Set aside.

4. Heat oven to 350 degrees. Roll pastry out to ⅛-inch thickness. Cut out circles with a round 2¼- to 3-inch cookie cutter. Place dough circles into nonstick mini-muffin pan cups. Gently push down the dough. Place 1 teaspoon cheesecake filling in each. Place a dark chocolate Hersey's Kiss in center of each. Top with 1 teaspoon cranberry relish.

5. Bake, 15 to 18 minutes. When cheesecake filling starts to rise and pastry slightly colors, they are done. Let cool completely, about 1 hour. Melt white chocolate in a saucepan over low heat; decoratively drizzle over the top.

Note: You will need 2 mini-muffin pans, each with 24 cups. Or make the tartlets in batches, waiting for the pan to cool completely between each.

Grandma Hazucha's Kolacky with Walnut Filling

Julie Hazucha Westbrook received an honorable mention for these cookies in 2012. She said both parts of the recipe can be halved.

Pastry:

4   sticks (1 pound) unsalted butter, softened

2   packages (8 ounces each) cream cheese or neufchatel, softened

4   cups flour

½   teaspoon salt

½   teaspoon baking powder

2   egg yolks
    Confectioners' sugar

Walnut filling:

½   cup milk

2   tablespoons unsalted butter

⅔   cup sugar

1   pound walnuts, finely chopped

1   tablespoon vanilla

Prep time:
1 hour, 10 minutes

Chill time: Overnight

Bake time: 12 to 15 minutes per batch

1. Place butter and cream cheese in a large mixing bowl. Cut butter into pieces; break up cream cheese. Add dry ingredients; work mixture with hands until dough is the size of peas. Add egg yolks; knead with hands again until well-blended. Divide dough into 5 pieces, wrap in wax paper and refrigerate overnight.

2. Heat oven to 350 degrees. To roll out dough, remove 2 portions from the refrigerator. Let soften, about 15 minutes. Open 1 package on a floured board; roll out with floured rolling pin very thin, about ⅛ inch. With pastry wheel, cut 2-inch rows across the dough; then cut diagonally across the rows to make slight diamond shapes, about 2 inches wide. Put pastry diamonds on ungreased cookie sheets.

3. Meanwhile, for walnut filling, slowly warm milk and butter in a medium saucepan over low heat, stirring frequently, until butter melts. Stir in sugar. Remove from heat; stir in walnuts and vanilla.

4. Put rounded ½ teaspoon walnut filling on each diamond. Fold over 2 opposite corners; to seal, wet inside of corners with a fingertip dipped in cold water; pinch corners together firmly so they do not open during baking. Bake until lightly browned, 12 to 15 minutes. Remove from cookie sheet; cool on a rack. Sprinkle with confectioners' sugar.

5. As the first bundle of dough is finished, take out another bundle to soften while the second bundle is being rolled out. Repeat until all bundles are used.

Yield: 50 to 60 cookies

Pictured on p. 74

Caramel Pecan Treasures

This first-place winner of the 1991 contest came from Elaine Rysner, who said she tried many different recipes, but this one was very unusual. Rysner suggested making the cookies small—about the diameter of a quarter. Use high-quality caramels and chocolate for best results.

1 cup (2 sticks) lightly salted butter, softened

¾ cup lightly packed light brown sugar

1 teaspoon vanilla

1¾ cups all-purpose flour

½ teaspoon baking powder

1 package (12 ounces) semisweet chocolate chips

1 tablespoon vegetable shortening

About 25–30 caramels, cut in half, rolled into balls

Finely chopped pecans

Prep time: 50 minutes

Bake time: 15 minutes per batch

1. Heat oven to 325 degrees. Have ungreased baking sheets ready.

2. Cream butter, sugar and vanilla in large mixer bowl until well mixed. Stir in flour and baking powder. (If kitchen is warm, refrigerate dough for a few minutes; dough should be firm enough to roll easily.) Shape scant teaspoonful of dough into balls about the size of a marble. Place on baking sheet, leaving about 2 inches between cookies. Flatten slightly.

3. Bake until golden, about 15 minutes. Transfer to wire racks to cool.

4. Melt chocolate chips with shortening in top of double boiler set over simmering water. Remove from heat.

5. Flatten caramel halves so they are the same diameter as the cookie. Put one caramel half on top of each cookie. (If necessary, use a dab of chocolate as "glue" to help caramel adhere to cookie.) Using a small metal spatula, spread melted chocolate thinly over top and sides of caramel and cookie to cover. Press chopped pecans onto tops of cookies. Let stand on a wire rack until chocolate firms (refrigerate if desired), about 20 minutes. Put into individual paper wrappers. Store in a cookie tin with a piece of wax paper between each layer.

Yield: 7 to 8 dozen cookies

Pictured on p. 19

Kolachkes

Shere Case said she grew up baking with her mother, and after Case had a family of her own, it became a tradition for the two to bake kolachkes together. Case fills these cookies, the recipe for which she got from a coworker, with a variety of jams, a cheese filling and a nut filling, and she said every member of her family has a favorite. The recipe can be halved. The kolachkes won third place in 1994.

Cookie:

2 cups (4 sticks) unsalted butter, softened

2 packages (3 ounces each) cream cheese, softened

3 cups all-purpose flour, sifted

6 tablespoons whipping cream
  Confectioners' sugar for rolling and sprinkling
  Jam, jelly or preserves of choice

Cream cheese filling (optional):

1 package (8 ounces) cream cheese, softened

1 egg yolk

½ cup confectioners' sugar

1 teaspoon pure vanilla extract

Nut filling (optional):

1 cup coarsely ground walnuts

2 tablespoons butter

⅓ cup granulated sugar

1 teaspoon pure vanilla extract

Prep time: 2½ hours

Chill time: Overnight

Bake time: 12 to 15 minutes per batch

1. Beat butter and cream cheese in large bowl of electric mixer until light. Beat in flour and cream until well mixed. Divide dough into 4 portions. Wrap each in plastic wrap and refrigerate overnight.

2. Heat oven to 350 degrees. Have ungreased baking sheets ready.

3. Sprinkle the work surface and the rolling pin generously with confectioners' sugar. Roll out 1 dough portion at a time to about ¼-inch thickness. Use a small (2-inch diameter), round cutter or glass to cut out cookies. Transfer to ungreased baking sheets, leaving 1 or 2 inches between each cookie. Make a small depression in the center of the cookies with your fingertip. Fill scantily with jam, jelly, preserves, cheese or nut filling. (If you use too much filling, it will run out onto the baking sheet.)

4. Bake until bottoms are lightly browned, 12 to 15 minutes. Cool on wire racks. Sprinkle generously with confectioners' sugar while still warm.

5. For cream cheese filling, beat together cream cheese, egg yolk, confectioners' sugar and pure vanilla extract until well mixed.

6. For nut filling, cook walnuts in butter with sugar and pure vanilla extract until nuts turn golden. Cool.

Kim Koenig said her 2013 first place prize-winning cookies were adapted from a recipe for Neapolitan cookies she used to make with her grandmother at Christmas. **In an unconventional method for a cookie,** all of the ingredients (except the cranberries and pistachios) get mixed together at the same time. The dough produces a crisp cookie.

Yield: About 120 cookies

2½ cups flour

1½ cups sugar

2 sticks (1 cup) unsalted butter, softened

1 egg

2½ teaspoons cinnamon

1½ teaspoons baking powder

1 teaspoon vanilla

½ teaspoon salt

1 cup dried cranberries, chopped

¾ cup pistachios, toasted, chopped

Decorative sugar

 **Prep time:** 20 minutes

Chill time: 4 hours

Bake time: 10 to 12 minutes per batch

Cranberry Coins

1. Heat oven to 350 degrees. Line cookie sheets with parchment paper or use a silicone mat.

2. With your mixer at low speed, beat all the ingredients (except the cranberries, pistachios and decorative sugar) until just mixed. Increase speed to medium; beat 3 minutes, scraping the bowl when necessary. Add cranberries and nuts; mix on low until just combined.

3. Divide dough in half; form into 2 logs about 1 inch in diameter. Wrap each in plastic wrap; refrigerate until firm, about 4 hours.

4. Remove wrap; slice logs crosswise into ⅛-inch-thick slices. Sprinkle with decorative sugar; place on parchment-lined cookie sheets. Bake until light brown, 10 to 12 minutes. Transfer cookies to wire racks to cool. Repeat with remaining cookies.

Dottie's Mexican Wedding Cookies

These cookies, which earned Kathleen Shelton an honorable mention in 1989, were part of a tradition her parents had with their friends, Dottie and Al Underwood, where they would get together every year for a meal of leftover Christmas turkey and cookies.

1 cup (2 sticks) butter, softened
½ cup confectioners' sugar
2 cups all-purpose flour
¼ teaspoon salt
1 teaspoon vanilla
1 cup chopped pecans
Confectioners' sugar for garnish

Prep time: 15 minutes

Bake time: 10 to 12 minutes per batch

1. Heat oven to 350 degrees. Cream butter and sugar until smooth in mixer bowl. Add flour, salt and vanilla and mix until blended. Mix in nuts.

2. Roll teaspoon-size pieces of dough in a ball and put onto an ungreased cookie sheet. Bake until light golden, 10 to 12 minutes. The cookie bottoms should be golden brown. Roll cookies in confectioners' sugar immediately after baking.

Yield: 2 ½ dozen cookies

Pictured on p. 67

1 cup (2 sticks) unsalted butter, softened
½ cup sifted confectioners' sugar
1 teaspoon vanilla
2 ¼ cups sifted cake flour
¼ teaspoon salt
¾ cup chopped pecans
Confectioners' sugar

Prep time: 20 minutes

Bake time: 7 minutes per batch

Melt Aways

This 1989 first-place recipe came from Chris Merrill, who topped more than 500 other entries. The cookies are slightly sweet and very buttery, so they melt in your mouth.

1. Heat oven to 450 degrees. Combine butter, confectioners' sugar and vanilla in mixing bowl.

2. Sift flour and salt together and gradually stir into butter mixture. Stir in chopped pecans.

3. Drop by heaping teaspoon onto an ungreased cookie sheet. Bake until peaks are very light brown, about 7 minutes. Transfer to cooling rack. While still warm (but not hot), use a sifter to sprinkle generously with confectioners' sugar.

Glazed Apricot–Almond Cookies

Nancy Vaziri won second place in 2011 for these pert little baubles. For the amaretto, you can substitute ⅛ teaspoon almond extract and ¼ cup plus 2 tablespoons milk.

Dough:

½ cup unsalted butter, room temperature

½ cup granulated sugar

⅛ teaspoon almond extract

¼ teaspoon salt

1 large egg

1¼ cups flour

1 cup dried apricots, coarsely chopped

⅓ cup almonds, toasted, coarsely chopped

Decoration:

2 cups confectioners' sugar

¼ cup plus 2 tablespoons amaretto

¼ cup chopped apricots

¼ cup sliced almonds

Prep time: 40 minutes

Chill time: 2 hours

Bake time: 12 minutes per batch

1. Beat the butter, sugar, almond extract and salt in a large bowl with an electric mixer until light and fluffy, about 2 minutes. Add egg; beat until combined. Add the flour; mix on low speed until combined. Stir in the apricots and almonds by hand. Transfer dough to a sheet of plastic wrap; shape into a log about 12 inches long and 1½ inches wide. Wrap dough in plastic wrap; refrigerate 2 hours. (Dough can be frozen at this point and baked later.)

2. Heat oven to 350 degrees. Cut the dough crosswise into ½-inch slices; place on parchment-lined baking sheets spaced evenly apart. Bake until the cookies are light brown around the edges, about 12 minutes.

3. To decorate, put the confectioners' sugar in a bowl; gradually stir in the amaretto until icing is of drizzling consistency. Spread about 1 tablespoon glaze on top of each cookie with an offset spatula to cover surface. Immediately sprinkle center of cookie with a few pieces of chopped apricots and almonds. Allow icing to set before serving, at least 1 hour.

Yield: 5 dozen cookies

Kolacky Dambrowski

These 2003 first-prize winners are traditional favorites from Antonette Clark's grandmother Veronica Dambrowski, who brought the recipe with her when she immigrated from Poland in 1921. Clark said she still makes the cookies with the rolling pin she inherited from her grandmother to get the right degree of thinness in the dough. She also said she keeps a variety of fillings on hand during the holiday season. (The recipe below calls for cream cheese filling.)

2   packages (8 ounces each) cream cheese, room temperature

2   teaspoons sugar

½   teaspoon vanilla extract

4   sticks (2 cups) butter, room temperature

3   cups flour
    Confectioners' sugar

Prep time: 45 minutes

Chill time: 4 hours

Bake time: 10 to 12 minutes per batch

1. For cream cheese filling, stir together ½ package (4 ounces) of the cream cheese, sugar and vanilla extract in a small bowl; set aside.

2. Beat together butter and remaining cream cheese in bowl of electric mixer on medium-high speed until fluffy, about 2 to 3 minutes. Add flour, 1 cup at a time, until well combined. Divide dough into thirds; wrap each third in plastic wrap. Refrigerate at least 4 hours.

3. Heat oven to 350 degrees. Remove 1 dough packet from refrigerator; roll to ⅛-inch thickness on a floured work surface. Cut into 1½-inch squares with a pizza cutter or knife. Fill each with about ½ teaspoon of the filling; fold two opposite corners of the dough over filling to almost meet in center. Place on greased cookie sheets.

4. Bake until golden, about 10 to 12 minutes. Transfer to flattened brown paper bags, which will absorb excess fat; cool completely. Repeat with remaining refrigerated dough in 2 more batches. Sprinkle cookies with confectioners' sugar.

Lime Pistachio Cookies with Cream Cheese Frosting

Dough:

1½ cups shelled, raw pistachios

2 sticks (1 cup) unsalted butter, softened

½ cup sugar

4 limes, zested, juiced, or to taste

1 teaspoon vanilla

½ teaspoon salt

Green food coloring

2¼ cups flour

Cream cheese frosting:

4 ounces cream cheese, room temperature

1 cup confectioners' sugar

1 tablespoon lime juice (about 1 whole lime)

1 teaspoon vanilla

Green food coloring

Decorative sprinkles

Prep time: 1 hour

Chill time: 1 hour

Bake time: 12 to 14 minutes per batch

1. Heat oven to 350 degrees. Place pistachios on a baking sheet; toast in the oven, about 10 minutes. When you start to smell them, they are ready. Cool completely; process in a food processor until just ground. Put aside.

2. Beat butter and sugar together in a bowl with an electric mixer or in a stand mixer until light and fluffy, about 3 minutes. Add lime zest and juice, vanilla and salt; mix slowly until well combined. Add 2 to 4 drops food coloring. Mix until uniform in color.

3. Add flour, mix well; add 1 cup ground pistachios. Wrap dough in plastic wrap; form a disc. Refrigerate, about 1 hour.

4. Meanwhile, for the frosting, mix cream cheese and confectioners' sugar in a bowl until well combined. Add lime juice, vanilla and a few drops of food coloring (tint to your desired green). Mix to blend.

5. Heat oven to 350 degrees again. Roll the dough out on a lightly floured surface to about ¼-inch thickness. Cut into trees with tree cookie cutters. Bake on ungreased cookie sheet, 12 to 14 minutes. Cool completely on racks.

6. Place cream cheese frosting in a plastic bag with a corner snipped off or use a piping bag with fine tip. Pipe frosting like garlands; sprinkle with remaining pistachios, colored sugar or decorations (or all three).

Sandy Szafranski's cookie recipe, which received an honorable mention in 2012, calls for the **zest and juice of 4 limes** for the dough, but the yield of those ingredients can vary depending on the limes. We had good results with 4 teaspoons zest and ¼ cup juice. If you cannot find raw pistachios, roasted and salted ones can sub. (You may want to reduce the added salt by ¼ teaspoon.)

Catherine Hall invented this recipe to toast Tu b'Shevat, the New Year for Trees. **"On Tu b'Shevat, we celebrate the bounty of nature by planting trees and tasting different kinds of fruit,"** she wrote. "We pay particular attention to the seven species listed in the Bible as being special products of the land of Israel: wheat, barley, olives, grapes, dates, figs and pomegranates." It won third place in 2012.

Middle East Fruit Bars

Crust:

2　cups flour

2　sticks (1 cup) unsalted butter

½　cup packed brown sugar

Filling:

1　cup figs, finely chopped

1　cup raisins

1　cup dates, sliced

1　cup pomegranate juice

Topping:

16　ounces cream cheese, softened

½　cup sugar

2　eggs

2　tablespoons pomegranate juice

Prep time: 30 minutes

Bake time: 45 minutes per batch

1. Heat oven to 350 degrees. For the crust, combine ingredients in a food processor or with a pastry blender until mixture resembles coarse crumbs. Pat mixture into the bottom of a well-greased 9-by-13-inch baking pan; bake, 20 minutes.

2. For the filling, combine ingredients in a saucepan; cook over medium heat, stirring occasionally, until most of the liquid is absorbed. Let cool slightly.

3. For the topping, whip ingredients together with an electric mixer or in a stand mixer until smooth and light. Spread fruit filling evenly over the hot crust. Pour topping over the filling. Bake, 25 minutes. Cool. Cut into bars; store in refrigerator.

Note: You can use a food processor or kitchen shears to chop the figs.

Yield: 5 to 6 dozen cookies

Pictured on p. 56

Nut Crescents

Mila Tomisek won first place in 1990 for this recipe, which has been in her family for more than 100 years. She started baking these cookies with her grandmother during World War I and sent them to a relative in the army. The small, buttery cookies were so fragile, they had to wrap them in a large box surrounded with popped corn, Tomisek said.

Dough:

2 cups (1 pound) unsalted butter or margarine, softened

6 tablespoons confectioners' sugar

2 large egg yolks

4 cups flour, sifted before measuring

1 cup ground or finely crushed almonds, pecans or walnuts

Topping:

2 large egg whites

1 cup ground or finely crushed almonds, pecans or walnuts

½ cup granulated sugar
Confectioners' sugar for sprinkling

1. Cream butter and confectioners' sugar in large mixer bowl until light and fluffy. Beat in egg yolks. Beat in flour and 1 cup ground nuts until mixed. (Dough can be refrigerated up to several days; soften slightly before shaping cookies.)

2. Heat oven to 350 degrees. Have ungreased baking sheets ready.

3. For topping, beat egg whites lightly with fork in shallow dish until frothy. Mix 1 cup nuts and granulated sugar in separate shallow dish.

4. Roll a generous teaspoon of the dough in the palm of your hands into a crescent shape. Dip top of crescent in egg white and then into nut-sugar mixture. Place crescents on baking sheets about 1 inch apart. Bake until bottoms are golden, 10 to 12 minutes. Cool on pan a few minutes, then transfer to wire racks to cool completely. Sprinkle lightly with confectioners' sugar before serving.

Prep time: 45 minutes

Bake time: 10 to 12 minutes per batch

HOLIDAY COOKIES

Yield: 10 to 12 dozen cookies

Pictured on p. 74

2 cups (4 sticks) lightly salted butter, softened

2 cups sugar

2 large eggs

Grated rind and juice of 1 lemon

4 cups all-purpose flour

1 teaspoon baking powder

Pinch salt

½ pound unblanched almonds, finely ground or grated

Colored sugars for garnish, optional

Prep time: 30 minutes

Chill time: 8 hours or overnight

Bake time: 8 to 10 minutes per batch

Oma's Almond Cookies

This 1991 second-place winner, from Judy M. Drux, makes very thin, crisp, delicate cookies. Drux submitted the recipe as a tribute to her husband's grandmother, who emigrated to the U.S. from Germany in 1923. The recipe was passed down as just a list of ingredients, but Drux added a few hints to make it easier for future cooks. The dough keeps well in the refrigerator if well-wrapped.

1. Cream butter and sugar in large bowl of electric mixer. Beat in eggs, 1 at a time. Beat in lemon rind and juice. Mix flour, baking powder and salt. Stir flour mixture and ground almonds into butter mixture to make a soft dough. Divide dough into quarters. Refrigerate dough, wrapped in wax paper, until firm, at least 8 hours or overnight.

2. Heat oven to 350 degrees. Have ungreased baking sheets ready.

3. Roll out 1 dough portion on lightly floured pastry cloth with a rolling pin covered with stocking, or roll between sheets of lightly floured wax paper to ⅛-inch thickness. Cut out with cookie cutters. Return dough to refrigerator if it gets too soft. Transfer to baking sheets, leaving 2 inches between each cookie. Sprinkle with colored sugar if desired.

4. Bake until very light brown at edges, 8 to 10 minutes. Transfer to wire racks to cool. Store in a covered tin.

Yield: 4½ to 5 dozen cookies

Orange Pecan Delights

Julie Foran won second place in 1997 for these pillow-soft cookies frosted with orange-scented icing and topped with a pecan half. They were the result of years of cookie preparation with a much-missed grandmother, Foran said, with whom she figured she made about 3,500 Christmas cookies over the years.

Dough:

3   cups flour

2   teaspoons baking powder

½   teaspoon baking soda

½   teaspoon salt

¾   cup unsalted butter, softened

1   cup brown sugar

½   cup granulated sugar

2   eggs

½   cup sour cream

1   tablespoon grated orange zest

1   cup chopped pecans

Frosting:

2   cups confectioners' sugar, sifted

2   teaspoons grated orange zest

⅛   teaspoon salt

3   tablespoons fresh orange juice

Pecan halves for garnish

Prep time: 25 minutes

Bake time: 10 to 14 minutes per batch

1. Heat oven to 375 degrees. For cookies, sift together flour, baking powder, baking soda and salt into large mixing bowl.

2. Cream together butter and sugars in bowl of electric mixer. Add eggs, one at a time, sour cream, orange zest and chopped nuts; mix together. Stir into flour mixture until smooth.

3. Drop dough by teaspoons onto greased cookie sheets; bake 10 to 14 minutes, or until golden.

4. For frosting, stir together confectioners' sugar, orange zest, salt and orange juice to taste. Spread frosting on warm, not hot, cookies. Top each cookie with a pecan half while icing is still soft.

From top: Orange Pecan Delights (opposite); Sour Cherry Rugelach (p. 101)

Yield: 2 dozen miniature tarts

Pictured on p. 140

Crust:

½ cup (1 stick) butter, softened

1 small package (3 ounces) cream cheese, softened

1 cup unsifted all-purpose flour

Filling:

1 large egg

¾ cup packed light brown sugar

1 tablespoon butter, melted

Pinch salt

¾ cup chopped pecans

Prep time: 30 minutes

Bake time: 25 minutes per batch

Pecan Tassies

This 1992 second-place winner came from Frances Marcinkiewicz, who said she makes more than 2,000 cookies each year to give to family, friends and co-workers. She added, however, that she always makes one batch of these miniature, rich pecan pies for herself.

1. Heat oven to 350 degrees. Have ready 2 miniature muffin tins with cups that measure about 2 inches across and ⅞ inch deep.

2. For crust, beat butter with cream cheese until smooth. Add flour and mix until a dough forms. Divide into 24 balls. With your fingers, press each ball into an ungreased muffin cup, taking care to make a smooth, even layer over the bottom and up the sides.

3. For filling, whisk egg in a medium bowl. Add sugar, butter and salt and mix well.

4. Spoon about ½ teaspoon chopped pecans into each crust. Add filling so it comes almost to the top of the cups, making sure it doesn't spill over. Sprinkle remaining pecans over the top.

5. Bake 15 minutes. Reduce oven to 250 degrees and continue to bake until crust is light brown at the edges, 10 minutes. Cool. When muffin tin is cool enough to handle, loosen cups from the sides of the tin and carefully transfer to a wire rack. Cool to room temperature.

Yield: 64 cookies

Pictured on p. 99

Sour Cherry Rugelach

Jean Linsner, who won first place in 1997 for this recipe, said these cookies are a "12-step program for intimidated would-be bakers." They are simple to prepare and temper their sweetness enough so you can eat several without overdosing on holiday cheer.

Dough:

1 cup (2 sticks) unsalted butter, room temperature

1 package (8 ounces) light cream cheese, room temperature

½ cup sugar

2¾ cups all-purpose flour

1 teaspoon salt

Filling:

¾ cup sugar

1 package (3.5 ounces) dried sour cherries or ⅔ cup, finely chopped

⅔ cup toasted walnuts, finely chopped

½ cup (1 stick) unsalted butter, melted

2 teaspoons cinnamon

1 teaspoon allspice

⅛ teaspoon salt

Glaze:

1 large egg, beaten
Granulated sugar

Prep time: 30 minutes

Chill time: 1 hour

Bake time: 20 minutes per batch

1. For dough, beat butter and cream cheese in large bowl of electric mixer until light. Add sugar; beat until fluffy. Mix in flour and salt. Gather dough into a ball; gently knead until smooth and flour is incorporated.

2. Divide dough into 8 equal pieces. Flatten into discs and wrap in plastic wrap. Refrigerate at least 1 hour

3. For filling, mix sugar, cherries, walnuts, melted butter, cinnamon, allspice and salt in medium bowl. Set aside. Heat oven to 350 degrees.

4. Unwrap dough discs and roll into 8-inch rounds on lightly floured surface. Spread 3 tablespoons of filling onto center of dough, leaving about a half-inch border. Using a pizza cutter or other straight blade, cut circle into 8 wedges.

5. Starting at wide end of each wedge, roll up each cookie tightly. Place tip side down on ungreased cookie sheets; bend into crescents. Repeat with remaining dough discs. Brush each crescent with beaten egg; sprinkle with sugar. Bake 20 minutes, or until rugelach are golden brown. Cool on wire racks.

Note: Nuts and cherries are easily chopped, separately, in a food processor. To keep cherries from sticking to blade, chop with about 1 tablespoon of the sugar.

Pistachio Cookies with Dark Chocolate Shell

This cookie was named an Editor's Pick in the 2012 contest after Tribune editor Joe Gray found himself coming back to it when the test kitchen was testing the winning recipes. This recipe came from Liza Antelo, who said her English mother made this cookie long ago and served it over tea as the family sat around the Christmas tree in the afternoon.

2 cups shelled pistachios, about 12 ounces

2 sticks (½ pound) unsalted butter, room temperature

⅓ cup confectioners' sugar

½ teaspoon salt

2 cups sifted flour

1 teaspoon vanilla

½ teaspoon almond extract

1 teaspoon water
   Granulated sugar for rolling

4 ounces dark chocolate

1 teaspoon vegetable oil

Prep time: 30 minutes

Bake time: 40 minutes per batch

1. Heat oven to 300 degrees. Toast pistachios in the oven on a baking sheet until fragrant, 6 to 7 minutes. Allow to cool. Process nuts (in a food processor) until finely ground but not yet a paste.

2. Use an electric mixer at high speed to beat the butter with the confectioners' sugar and salt. Beat until light and fluffy. Lower the speed; gradually add flour until just blended. Do not overbeat. Add vanilla, almond extract and water. Gently mix in pistachios. Form into a ball.

3. Roll tablespoons of dough into balls. Pour about ½ cup granulated sugar into a shallow dish; roll and coat the balls in the sugar. Place the balls about 2 inches apart on greased or parchment-lined cookie sheets. Press down lightly on each cookie with the bottom of a glass to flatten slightly.

4. Bake on the top and middle shelves of the oven, about 20 minutes. Switch the sheets around; bake until cookies are slightly browned, 20 minutes. Cool cookies on baking sheet, 10 minutes.

5. Meanwhile, in a double-boiler, gently melt chocolate with the oil. (The chocolate also can be melted in a bowl in the microwave.) Dip cookies in chocolate; transfer to wire rack to cool. Transfer to wax paper; refrigerate to cool completely and set the chocolate.

From top left: White Chocolate Chip Cookies with Dried Cherries (opposite); Grandma's Christmas Date–Nut Bars (p. 193); Kolacky Dambrowski (p. 90)

White Chocolate Chip Cookies with Dried Cherries

Cynthia McKinley created this cookie to satisfy her craving for white chocolate, and it claimed second prize in 2003. She came upon the recipe while playing around with what she described as a "silly" pseudo-Mrs. Fields' cookie recipe her friends passed around. These big, hearty cookies have lots of different textures that work together.

2½	cups uncooked old-fashioned rolled oats
2	cups flour
1	teaspoon baking soda
1	teaspoon baking powder
½	teaspoon salt
2	sticks (1 cup) butter
1	cup granulated sugar
1	cup packed light brown sugar
2	eggs
1	teaspoon vanilla extract
1	package (12 ounces) white chocolate chips
1½	cups chopped walnuts
1	cup dried cherries or cranberries

Prep time: 25 minutes

Bake time: 10 to 12 minutes per batch

1. Heat oven to 375 degrees; process oats in a food processor to a fine powder. Combine oatmeal, flour, baking soda, baking powder and salt in a medium bowl; set aside.

2. Beat together butter and sugars in bowl of an electric mixer on medium speed until combined; beat in eggs and vanilla until fluffy. Reduce speed to low; add dry ingredients, about ½ cup at a time. Stir in chips, walnuts and dried cherries.

3. Drop by tablespoon on greased baking sheets. Bake in batches until golden, about 10 to 12 minutes, rotating baking sheet after 5 minutes. Remove to wire racks; cool.

Yield: About 6 dozen cookies

Baba's Cream Cheese Kolacky

This recipe was handed down to Emily Dressel by her grandmother, Baba, and won the 2008 contest. Dressel said Baba was one of the last war brides to flee Czechoslovakia before the Communists closed the borders, in 1947, and she came to the U.S. with all of her recipes stored only in her memory. These cookies are simple and elegant with a tender cream cheese dough and sweetly tart apricot filling.

1 bag (10 ounces) dried apricots

½ cup granulated sugar

2 sticks (1 cup) butter, room temperature

1 package (8 ounces) cream cheese, room temperature

2 cups flour

Confectioners' sugar

Prep time: 45 minutes

Soaking time: Overnight

Chill time: 4 hours

Bake time: 17 minutes per batch

1. Place apricots in medium saucepan; cover with water. Soak overnight. Heat the apricots and water to a boil in medium saucepan over high heat; reduce heat to low. Simmer, stirring often with fork to mash and adding water if needed, until smooth and thick, about 10 minutes. (If necessary, you can chop finely with a knife or process about 1 minute in a food processor or chopper.) Add the granulated sugar, stirring until it dissolves. Cool completely.

2. Blend together the butter and cream cheese in a large bowl; gradually blend in flour, using hands once the dough has begun to form, until it can be shaped into a ball (this may be more or less than 2 cups). Refrigerate 4 hours or overnight.

3. Heat oven to 350 degrees. Divide dough into thirds. Roll out each third on a floured board into a 12-by-8-inch rectangle, ⅛ to ¼ inch thick. Cut into 2-inch squares with a pizza cutter. Place ½ to ¾ teaspoon of the apricot filling in the middle of each square. Fold each corner into middle; pinch together. (Moisten fingers with cold water if dough does not stick.)

4. Place cookies on ungreased cookie sheets; bake until golden, about 17 minutes per batch. Cool on wire rack; sprinkle with confectioners' sugar.

From left: Baba's Cream Cheese Kolacky (opposite); Dorie's Dark and Stormies (p. 153); Irv's Mandelbrot (p. 191)

Yield: 68 cookies

Jelly Thumbprints (Hussarn Grapsen)

Gayle Fross won second place in 2005 with this recipe, which she said was created by her great-great-aunt in Vienna who was an official baker for Austrian royalty. Legend has it that this was the king's favorite cookie, Fross said.

4   sticks (2 cups) butter, softened
6   egg yolks, room temperature
1   cup sugar
4   cups flour
   Zest of 1 lemon
¼   teaspoon salt
3   tablespoons grape jelly

Prep time: 45 minutes

Bake time: 15 minutes per batch

Cooling time: 30 minutes

1. Heat oven to 350 degrees. Combine the butter, egg yolks and sugar in a large bowl; beat with a mixer on medium-high speed until light and fluffy, about 3 minutes. Reduce speed to low; slowly beat in flour, zest and salt just until blended.

2. Roll scant teaspoonfuls of dough into tiny balls; place balls on lightly greased baking sheets. Make indentions in balls with the smallest end of a melon baller or your finger or thumb dipped in flour, being careful not to poke through the dough.

3. Fill indentations with jelly. Bake until edges begin to lightly brown, about 15 minutes. Remove from sheet to wire rack; cool 30 minutes.

Rita Allan's Strudel

Randi Sagall received an honorable mention in 2006 for this cookie named as a tribute to her mother. "Although her grandchildren will only see their grandmother in photos, they have known her for years through the recipes that make our home so special," Sagall wrote.

1 stick (½ cup) butter, room temperature

3 ounces cream cheese, room temperature

1 cup flour

1 jar (12 ounces) apricot preserves

¾ cup sweetened flaked coconut

1 bag (about 10 ounces) chopped pecans

3 tablespoons confectioners' sugar

Prep time: 35 minutes

Chill time: 1 hour

Bake time: 25 to 30 minutes per batch

1. Stir together the butter and cream cheese in a medium bowl until well combined; stir in flour. Cover; refrigerate at least 1 hour.

2. Heat oven to 350 degrees. Divide dough into 3 equal pieces. Roll out each piece on a floured surface into an 8-inch square. Spread one-third of the apricot preserves over each square; top with coconut and pecans. Roll up carefully, like a jelly roll, into a log; pinch ends together. Transfer the 3 logs to 1 large or 2 small greased or parchment-lined cookie sheets, seam side down.

3. Bake until lightly golden, 25 to 30 minutes; cool on a rack. Sprinkle with confectioners' sugar. Slice into ½-inch pieces.

Yield: 3 dozen cookies

1   stick (½ cup) butter

1   cup confectioners' sugar, sifted

½   cup granulated sugar

1   egg yolk, beaten

¾   teaspoon vanilla extract

⅛   teaspoon almond extract

1¼ cups flour

1   teaspoon baking soda

1   teaspoon cream of tartar

1   tablespoon light corn syrup

1   cup finely chopped pistachios

½   cup orange juice

2   teaspoons cornstarch

1   tablespoon fresh lemon juice

1   package (8 ounces) cream cheese

¼   teaspoon orange zest

¼   teaspoon lemon zest

3½ cups fresh mixed fruit, diced

Prep time: 55 minutes

Chill time:
2 hours, 30 minutes

Bake time: 10 minutes per batch

Fresh Fruit Jewels

1. Place butter, ½ cup of the confectioners' sugar and ¼ cup of the granulated sugar in bowl of electric mixer; beat until light and fluffy. Add egg yolk, ¼ teaspoon of the vanilla extract and almond extract. Beat well. Mix flour, baking soda and cream of tartar in small bowl; stir into butter mixture. Shape into 2-by-1-inch logs; wrap in plastic. Refrigerate until firm, at least 2 hours.

2. Heat oven to 350 degrees; unwrap logs. Brush each log on all sides with corn syrup. Spread pistachios in single layer on baking sheet. Roll logs in pistachios until well coated. Cut logs into ¼-inch slices. Bake on greased baking sheets until slightly brown around edges, about 10 minutes. Remove with spatula; cool on wire racks.

3. Combine 1 tablespoon of the orange juice with cornstarch in small bowl; set aside. Heat remaining orange juice, lemon juice and remaining ¼ cup granulated sugar to boiling; stir in orange-cornstarch mixture. Cook over medium heat until thickened to a glaze consistency, about 2 minutes; set aside.

4. Beat cream cheese, remaining ½ cup of confectioners' sugar, orange zest, lemon zest and remaining ½ teaspoon of vanilla extract with an electric mixer on medium speed until fluffy. Spread 1 teaspoon of the mixture on each cookie. Decorate with fruit pieces. Brush ¼ teaspoon of orange glaze over each cookie with pastry brush; chill until glaze sets, 30 minutes. Cover with plastic wrap; keep refrigerated until 15 minutes before serving time.

These unique jewel cookies, so named because "they're pretty and sparkly," Nancy Vaziri wrote, earned the top prize in 2002. Vaziri said **the cookies, filling and glaze can be made up to one week ahead,** and the fruit can be prepped one day before you plan to serve the cookies. She used strawberries, oranges, kiwi and blueberries to top the cookies brought in for judging but said she has also decorated them with raspberries, pineapple, pomegranate seeds and grapes.

From top left: Cucidati (opposite); Hazelnut-Coffee Oatmeal Cookies (p. 26); Sirapskakor (p. 52)

Cucidati (Sicilian Fig Cookies)

This 2004 second-place winner came from Eilene Guarnera, who said her aunt used to deliver packages of cucidati to the family on Christmas Eve. She noted that it's important to measure the sifted flour before preparing this dough.

Filling:

1 package (12 ounces) dried figs, soaked in water 45 minutes, stemmed, diced

1 box (15 ounces) golden raisins

1 cup chopped walnuts
   Zest from 1 orange

¾ cup orange marmalade

¾ cup sugar

½ cup honey

2 teaspoons cinnamon

2 teaspoons nutmeg

Dough:

4 cups sifted flour

2½ teaspoons baking powder

2 sticks (1 cup) butter, room temperature

1 cup sugar

1 teaspoon vanilla

3 eggs

Frosting:

1 cup confectioners' sugar

2 tablespoons milk

½ teaspoon vanilla

3 tablespoons multicolored decorative sprinkles

Prep time: 45 minutes
Bake time: 10 to 12 minutes per batch

1. Heat oven to 375 degrees. For filling, combine figs, raisins, walnuts, zest, marmalade, sugar, honey, cinnamon and nutmeg in a food processor. Process until ingredients are finely chopped and mixture is a thick consistency; set aside.

2. For dough, sift together sifted flour and baking powder; set aside. Beat butter and sugar with a mixer on medium-high speed. Add vanilla. Add flour mixture, alternating with eggs 1 at a time, until combined. Roll out dough on floured board; cut into 2½-inch circles, using a biscuit cutter or the floured rim of a glass.

3. Add small amount of filling down the middle of each circle; fold 1 side over filling, then fold second side over, overlapping slightly. Press down lightly, spreading with a little water to seal. Bake on lightly greased baking sheet until light brown around edges, about 10 to 12 minutes. Cool completely on rack.

4. For frosting, combine confectioners' sugar, milk and vanilla. Brush frosting over cookies; sprinkle with candies.

Butterchews

Claudia Greene said she remembers how as a child, she used to sneak butterchews from the freezer stash of holiday cookies her mother baked each fall. The tiny squares combining butter, pecans and coconut offer unexpected layers of texture and flavor. They earned an honorable mention in 2002.

1½ sticks (¾ cup) butter or margarine

3 tablespoons granulated sugar

1 cup flour

2¼ cups packed dark brown sugar

3 eggs, separated

1 cup chopped pecans

¾ cup sweetened coconut flakes

¼ cup confectioners' sugar, optional

🕐 **Prep time:** 15 minutes

Bake time: 42 to 45 minutes per batch

Cooling time: 45 minutes

1. Heat oven to 350 degrees. Beat butter and granulated sugar in bowl of electric mixer at medium speed. Stir in flour to form thick dough. Pat mixture into a greased 13-by-9-inch baking pan. Bake until light brown around edges, 12 to 15 minutes; set aside.

2. Mix brown sugar and egg yolks in same bowl of electric mixer at low speed. Mix in nuts and coconut; set aside. Beat the egg whites in clean bowl of electric mixer until thick and frothy but not stiff, about 4 minutes. Gently fold whites into nut mixture. Spread over baked layer.

3. Bake until set, about 30 minutes. Cool pan completely on wire rack, about 45 minutes. Cut into 1-by-1-inch squares. Sprinkle with confectioners' sugar, if desired.

Yield: 60 pieces

Macadamia Nut Toffee

New York pastry master Francois Payard wrote in his cookbook, "Simply Sensational Desserts," that he is "wild about caramel." This particular confection is served without a chocolate topping. You may substitute any nut as desired.

1⅔   cups sugar

1¼   cups whipping cream

2   tablespoons light corn syrup

2¾   cups finely chopped macadamias or other nuts

🕐 **Prep time:** 10 minutes

Bake time: 20 minutes per batch

Cooling time: 30 minutes

1. Combine sugar, cream and corn syrup in a heavy saucepan. Heat to a boil over medium-high heat, stirring to dissolve the sugar. Insert a candy thermometer into the syrup; boil without stirring until mixture reaches 284 degrees, about 20 minutes.

2. Remove from heat; stir in nuts. Spread toffee onto buttered baking sheet with sides, working quickly. Let cool in the pan on a rack, 30 minutes. Break into irregular pieces. Store in an airtight container in a cool, dry place for up to 2 weeks.

From left: Coconut Cranberry Pinwheels (p. 130); Mexican Mice (p. 64); Hazelnut Chocolate Fingers (opposite)

Yield: About 4 dozen cookies

Hazelnut Chocolate Fingers

Cindy Beberman, who said her mother taught her to bake while they lived in rural Kansas, won third place for this recipe in the 2000 contest.

1 cup shelled hazelnuts
2¼ cups flour
¼ teaspoon salt
2 sticks (1 cup) unsalted butter, softened
⅓ cup sugar
2 teaspoons vanilla extract
1¼ cups milk chocolate chips
⅛ bar paraffin, optional

Prep time: 50 minutes

Bake time: 15 minutes per batch

Chill time: 10 minutes

1. Heat oven to 350 degrees. Toast hazelnuts on baking sheet 15 minutes. Remove from oven; rub while still warm in clean towel to remove most of skins. Place in food processor; process until finely ground. Mix together hazelnuts, flour and salt in small bowl; set aside.

2. Beat butter, sugar and vanilla in bowl of electric mixer until light and fluffy. Add flour-hazelnut mixture; mix until well combined. Roll tablespoon of dough between palms, forming 2-inch-long cylinders. Place on ungreased baking sheet. Bake until golden brown, about 15 minutes. Cool on wire rack.

3. Melt chocolate and paraffin in double boiler, stirring constantly, over simmering water. Remove from heat. Dip half of each cookie into chocolate, letting excess drip off. Place on cookie sheet lined with wax paper. Chill until chocolate sets, about 10 minutes.

From left: Cherry Pie Almond Thumbprints (opposite); Grandma's Walnut Horns (p. 122); Mutti's Butter Cookies (p. 41).

Cherry Pie Almond Thumbprints

This recipe from Cheryl Stritzel McCarthy won third place in the 2009 contest.

Dough:

⅔ cup butter

⅓ cup sugar

2 eggs, separated

½ teaspoon vanilla

½ teaspoon almond extract

½ teaspoon salt

1½ cups flour

1 cup finely chopped almonds

Sliced almonds, for garnish

Filling:

2 cups pitted tart cherries, thawed, drained

⅓ cup sugar

1 tablespoon cornstarch

½ teaspoon vanilla

½ teaspoon almond extract

1 tablespoon butter

Prep time: 40 minutes

Bake time: 14 minutes per batch

1. Heat oven to 350 degrees. Combine butter and sugar in large bowl; beat with electric mixer until creamy. Beat in egg yolks, vanilla and almond extract. Stir together salt and flour in small bowl. Add to butter mixture; beat until smooth.

2. Shape dough into 1-inch balls. Beat egg whites in small bowl until frothy; dip cookies in egg white to coat. Dip cookies in nuts to coat. Place balls 2 inches apart on parchment-lined cookie sheets. Press an indentation in the middle of each cookie with your thumb. Bake until lightly browned on bottoms, rotating pan once, about 14 minutes per batch. Remove to wire rack; cool.

3. Meanwhile, for filling, combine cherries, sugar and cornstarch in a large saucepan; heat over medium-high heat, stirring occasionally, to a boil. Boil, stirring, 1 minute. Remove from heat. Add vanilla, almond extract and butter. Cool. Fill each cookie with a tiny scoop of cherry filling. Garnish with an almond slice, if desired.

Yield: About 8 dozen cookies

Nut Horn Kolacky

This recipe was passed down to Lorraine O'Malley from her grandmother, and received an honorable mention in 2007.

Dough:

1 cup sour cream

2 packages (¼ ounce each) quick-rise yeast

6 cups flour

4 sticks (2 cups) butter, chilled

1 teaspoon salt

3 eggs, beaten

1 teaspoon vanilla

Filling:

1¼ cups finely ground walnuts

1¼ cups granulated sugar

½ cup confectioners' sugar

Prep time: 50 minutes

Chill time: 4 hours

Bake time: 15 minutes per batch

1. Heat the sour cream in a saucepan over medium heat just until warm; stir in the yeast. Set aside, keep the mixture warm (between 120 and 130 degrees).

2. Meanwhile, combine the flour, butter and salt in a large bowl; blend together with a pastry blender until coarse crumbs form. Add beaten eggs, one at a time, stirring after each addition. Add the sour cream mixture and vanilla; mix well with a mixer on low speed.

3. Knead the dough in the bowl until it begins to look glossy but is still sticky, about 5 minutes. Cover; refrigerate 3 hours.

4. Roll dough into 1-inch balls. Return the balls to the bowl, placing wax paper between layers. Cover bowl with wax paper; refrigerate until chilled, about 1 hour.

5. Heat the oven to 350 degrees. For filling, mix walnuts and sugars in a small bowl. Remove a dozen balls at a time from the refrigerator. Place one ball on a surface lightly covered with confectioners' sugar; roll out to a 3- to 4-inch circle. Place a heaping teaspoon of the filling in center; fold dough over filling, pressing the edges and forming a crescent shape. Place on ungreased cookie sheets; bake until golden on top, about 15 minutes. Cool on wire racks.

Yield: 15 cookies

Mor Mors Coconut Cookies

This delicate, macaroon-like cookie with a hint of almond flavoring was an honorable mention for Jan Schippits in 2003. "Mors mors" translates to mother's mother, or grandmother, in Swedish. The recipe was passed down from Schippits' Swedish grandmother, who worked as a cook in Manhattan for the Vanderbilt family when she arrived in New York in 1908.

½ cup sugar

1 egg

2 cups sweetened, shredded coconut

2 tablespoons flour

½ teaspoon almond extract

Prep time: 10 minutes

Bake time: 10 minutes per batch

1. Heat oven to 350 degrees. Whisk together sugar and egg until smooth; stir in coconut, flour and almond extract. Mix well.

2. Drop dough by teaspoon on a greased baking sheet. Bake until edges are lightly browned, about 10 minutes. Transfer to wire racks; cool.

Grandma's Walnut Horns

Beth Grabowski said she reminisces about her grandmas whenever she bakes, and her secret weapon is her great-grandma's rolling pin carried over to the U.S. from Russia. She said the dough for these cookies, which won first place in 2009, must be prepared at least six hours ahead of baking, and the recipe can be doubled.

2 sticks (1 cup) unsalted butter, softened

2 cups flour

¾ cup sour cream

1 egg yolk, beaten

1 cup light brown sugar

1 cup ground walnuts

1 teaspoon cinnamon
Confectioners' sugar, optional

Prep time: 60 minutes

Chill time: 6 hours

Bake time: 13 to 18 minutes per batch

1. Mix butter with flour in medium bowl by hand or with electric mixer. Add sour cream to egg yolk; mix. Add to flour mixture; beat until sticky dough forms. Divide dough into four sections; wrap individually in plastic wrap. Refrigerate at least 6 hours.

2. Heat oven to 350 degrees. Mix brown sugar, walnuts and cinnamon in a bowl. Take one section of dough from the refrigerator; sprinkle flour on both sides of the dough. Roll the dough out on a lightly floured surface to about ⅛-inch thickness. Spread a thin layer of filling on the dough, almost to the edges. Cut the dough with a pizza cutter into quarters; cut into 3 to 4 wedges per quarter.

3. Starting at the widest end, gently roll up each wedge like a crescent roll. Place on greased, light-colored cookie sheets with the tail end of the dough tucked under; bake 13 to 18 minutes per batch. Cool; sprinkle with confectioners' sugar.

Pecan Pie Cookies

Barbara Marine's 2006 third-place winners have a center of pecans surrounded by a soft cookie. Marine said she adapted the recipe from one she received from a student when she was teaching first grade.

Filling:

½ cup confectioners' sugar

½ stick (¼ cup) butter, softened

3 tablespoons dark corn syrup

½ cup chopped pecans

Dough:

2 sticks (1 cup) butter, softened

½ cup sugar

½ cup dark corn syrup

2 eggs, separated

2½ cups flour

Prep time: 30 minutes

Chill time: 2 hours

Bake time: 17 minutes per batch

1. For the filling, heat the sugar, butter and corn syrup to a boil in a small saucepan over medium heat; remove from heat. Stir in pecans. Set aside to cool, 10 minutes. Transfer to a food storage bag. Press to flatten; seal. Refrigerate at least 2 hours.

2. Meanwhile, for cookies, beat butter and sugar together with a mixer on low speed until well combined. Beat in corn syrup and egg yolks until combined. Stir in flour gradually. Transfer to a food storage bag; press to flatten. Seal; chill 1 hour.

3. Heat oven to 375 degrees. Cut pecan mixture into 36 equal pieces; set aside. Whisk the egg whites in a small bowl until foamy; set aside. Form 1-inch balls of dough; place on greased or parchment-lined cookie sheet, 2 inches apart. Brush tops lightly with egg whites. Bake cookies 7 minutes per batch.

4. Remove cookie sheet from oven. Press 1 piece of the pecan filling into the center of each cookie. Return to oven; bake until light brown, about 10 minutes per batch. Cool on racks.

Yield: 4 dozen tartlets

2   sticks (1 cup) plus 2 tablespoons unsalted butter, softened

6   ounces cream cheese, softened

2   cups flour

1¼ cups chopped pecans

2   large eggs

1½ cups light brown sugar

2   teaspoons vanilla extract

2   tablespoons Bourbon, optional

½   teaspoon kosher salt

48 pecan halves, optional
    Chocolate drizzle, see note, or confectioners' sugar

🕐 **Prep time:** 1 hour

Chill time: 1 hour

Bake time: 25 minutes per batch

Pecan Dollies

1. Beat 2 sticks of the butter and cream cheese in bowl of an electric mixer on medium speed until light and fluffy, about 3 minutes. Stir in the flour with a wooden spoon; lightly mix just until flour is incorporated. Divide dough into 4 equal portions; shape into 6-inch logs. Wrap logs in plastic wrap; refrigerate at least 1 hour.

2. Cut each log into 12 half-inch pieces; place in oiled mini-muffin tins. Press dough into the bottoms and up sides of each cup; refrigerate until ready to fill. (Repeat in batches, if necessary.)

3. Heat oven to 325 degrees. Divide chopped pecans among pastry cups. Beat eggs, brown sugar, vanilla, remaining 2 tablespoons butter, Bourbon and salt with an electric mixer on medium speed. Fill each pastry cup ¾ full with this mixture; top with a pecan half, if desired

4. Bake until filling is set, about 25 minutes. Cool pans on wire rack 20 minutes; remove cups from pan. Cool. Drizzle with chocolate, if desired, or dust with confectioners' sugar.

Note: To make chocolate drizzle, place ½ cup semisweet chocolate pieces and 1 teaspoon shortening in microwave-safe bowl; heat in the microwave on medium heat until melted, 1 to 2 minutes; stir with fork until smooth and shiny. Dip fork tines in chocolate; drizzle randomly over cookies. Allow chocolate to harden before storing or packaging.

Tracy Smodilla said she created this cookie recipe by combining what she liked best about her family's **Southern pecan pie recipe** with the **Polish nut cups** her mother-in-law made. "Besides the feeling of family that I get when baking this cookie, I just love the way it looks when it's presented," she said. Smodilla won second place in the 2002 contest for this recipe.

Yield: About 3 dozen cookies

Mexican Pecan Cookies

The 1996 third-place winner was Marilyn Cahill of Chicago, with her recipe for Mexican pecan cookies. She wrote that she learned the recipe during a trip to Mexico City and a visit to the home of Eva Trejo. "One thing that unites people all over the world (beside eating) is creating what to eat. We spent the morning mixing cookie dough, melting chocolate and chopping pecans for holiday cookies. Because Mrs. Trejo had fewer modern appliances such as I am used to, I resorted to the old pecans-in-a-plastic-bag crushed-by-a-hammer and beating 300 strokes, with me counting in Spanish and Mrs. Trejo practicing her English numbers. Try doing that without having a few laughs... I plan on making these holiday cookies every year, although I don't know if I will ever have as much fun cooking in English as I did in Spanish."

1 cup sugar
½ cup each, softened: unsalted butter, lard, see note
1 egg yolk
1 teaspoon vanilla
2¼ cups all-purpose flour
¾ teaspoon cinnamon
¼ teaspoon anise seed, finely crushed
   Pinch salt
½ cup finely chopped pecans

Prep time: 15 minutes

Bake time: 22–25 minutes per batch

1. Heat oven to 350 degrees. Beat ¾ cup of the sugar, butter and lard in large bowl of electric mixer on high speed until light and fluffy, about 3 minutes. Add egg yolk and vanilla; beat until smooth. Beat in flour, cinnamon, anise seed and salt until well mixed. Stir in pecans.

2. Roll walnut-size pieces of dough between palms to make round balls. Put remaining ¼ cup sugar in pie plate; roll dough balls in sugar. Place balls 5 inches apart on ungreased cookie sheet. Press each ball with bottom of a glass dipped in sugar to about ¼-inch thickness.

3. Bake 10 minutes. Reduce oven to 300 degrees and continue baking until lightly browned, 12 to 15 minutes. Remove to cooling rack.

Note: An additional ½ cup butter can be substituted for the lard. Also, you may bake the cookies at a constant 325 degrees; cooking time should be about the same.

Yield: About 3 dozen cookies

Coconut Cranberry Pinwheels

Dough:

1 cup flour
¼ cup yellow cornmeal
½ teaspoon grated nutmeg
¼ teaspoon baking soda
¼ teaspoon baking powder
¼ teaspoon salt
6 tablespoons unsalted butter, softened
3 ounces cream cheese, softened
½ cup granulated sugar
1 large egg yolk
1 cup sweetened flaked coconut

Filling:

1 cup dried sweetened cranberries
1 cup water
¾ cup sweetened flaked coconut
3 tablespoons granulated sugar
⅓ cup turbinado sugar for coating, see note

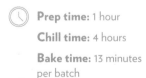 **Prep time:** 1 hour

Chill time: 4 hours

Bake time: 13 minutes per batch

1. For dough, combine flour, cornmeal, nutmeg, baking soda, baking powder and salt in small bowl; set aside. Beat together butter, cream cheese and granulated sugar in bowl of electric mixer until light and fluffy. Add egg yolk; beat until combined. Add flour mixture on low speed; mix until dough forms. Add coconut; mix until combined. Scrape dough from bowl onto wax paper. Wrap; chill in refrigerator until firm, about 1 hour.

2. Meanwhile, for filling, combine cranberries, water, coconut and granulated sugar in small saucepan. Heat to boil; reduce heat, cook until almost all water is absorbed, about 20 minutes. Place in food processor or blender; purée until thick paste forms. Refrigerate to cool.

3. After dough has chilled, roll into 8-by-15-inch rectangle about ¼ inch thick on lightly floured wax paper. Spread cranberry mixture evenly over dough. Roll up from long end into tight cylinder. Sprinkle turbinado sugar onto wax paper; roll dough to coat cylinder. Wrap in wax paper. Place on baking sheet; refrigerate until firm, about 3 hours. (Dough may be frozen at this point if making several days in advance. Thaw in refrigerator before continuing.)

4. Heat oven to 350 degrees. Slice cookies about ¼ inch thick; place on greased baking sheet about 1 inch apart. Bake until bottoms are slightly browned, about 13 minutes. Cool on wire rack.

Note: Turbinado sugar, sometimes called "raw" sugar, is a coarsely granulated tan-colored sugar sold in most supermarkets.

Robert Hafey won the 2000 contest for these pinwheels, which have a nice, mild cranberry flavor and pleasant crunch. Hafey's mother used to make date pinwheels, which he loved but found really sweet. Instead, he used dried sweetened cranberries combined with sweetened flaked coconut and added a little nutmeg.

Yield: 18 cookies

½ cup tropical mixed dried fruit, chopped

3 tablespoons sweetened coconut, finely chopped

2 tablespoons crystallized ginger, finely chopped

1 tablespoon rum or 1 teaspoon vanilla

Grated zest from 1 lime

Juice from 2 limes

1 egg, separated

½ stick (¼ cup) unsalted butter, softened

¼ cup granulated sugar

¼ teaspoon ginger

¼ teaspoon allspice

¼ teaspoon nutmeg

⅛ teaspoon salt

⅔ cup flour

¼ cup turbinado or granulated sugar

¼ cup chopped, slivered almonds

Prep time: 1 hour

Standing time: 30 minutes

Bake time: 15 minutes per batch

Cooling time: 15 minutes

Tropical Nuevo Latino Cookies

"If a cookie recipe created in the 21st century were placed in a time capsule for posterity, what would it reflect about our culture today?" That is what 2007 contest winner Nancy Vaziri wrote in her entry essay about these cookies, which she said "fuse Hispanic flavors with traditional American cooking traditions." The recipe calls for dried tropical fruit mixtures, crystallized ginger and turbinado sugar.

1. Heat the oven to 375 degrees. Stir together dried fruit, coconut, ginger, rum, half of the lime zest and the lime juice in a small bowl; let stand 30 minutes.

2. Meanwhile, beat egg yolk, butter, granulated sugar, ginger, allspice, nutmeg and salt with a mixer on medium speed until light and fluffy, about 3 minutes. Add the flour in 2 parts, beating just until combined.

3. Divide dough in half; roll each half into two 10-by-1-inch logs. Transfer to a large baking sheet lined with parchment paper. Slightly press each log to flatten dough into 2-inch widths. Press a 1-inch-wide channel down the center of each log; set aside.

4. Whisk the egg white in a medium bowl; brush lightly over each log with a pastry brush; set remaining egg white aside. Combine the turbinado sugar, remaining zest and the almonds in a small bowl. Whisk in 1 tablespoon of the reserved egg white; set aside.

5. Place the fruit mixture into log channels with a teaspoon, pressing lightly with fingers to secure mixture. Top fruit mixture with teaspoons of the sugar mixture, spreading evenly with a knife to coat logs. Bake until topping is crisp and lightly golden, about 15 minutes. Cool on sheets 15 minutes. Remove logs to cutting board; slice diagonally into 2-inch cookies with a sharp knife.

Yield: 5 dozen cookies

Orange Macadamia Cookies in Chocolate

These cookies from Cynthia Craven Beberman earned an honorable mention in 2001. They look like classic New York black-and-whites, and tasters will find they have a nice, nutty cookie and a hint of tart orange flavor. Paraffin, available at some supermarkets and hardware stores, is an edible wax that gives chocolate a bright sheen.

1½ cups macadamia nuts
½   cup sweetened, flaked coconut
2   sticks (1 cup) unsalted butter, softened
1   cup superfine sugar, or sugar processed in the food processor
½   teaspoon salt
    Zest from 2 oranges
1   egg
1   egg yolk
2   teaspoons vanilla extract
2½ cups flour
1   cup semisweet chocolate chips
1   cup milk chocolate chips
1   1-inch square paraffin, optional

Prep time: 45 minutes

Chill time: 1 hour

Bake time: 7 to 9 minutes per batch

Freezing time: 25 minutes

1. Heat oven to 350 degrees. Place macadamia nuts on a baking sheet; place coconut in shallow baking pan. Toast, stirring often, until golden brown, about 7 minutes. Remove from oven; let cool. Grind nuts. You should have 1 cup. Set nuts and coconut aside.

2. Place butter, sugar and salt in the bowl of an electric mixer. Beat until light and fluffy, about 5 minutes. Mix in nuts and orange zest. Beat in egg, egg yolk and vanilla until well blended. Beat in flour on low speed just until mixed. Stir in coconut. Cover dough with plastic wrap; refrigerate 1 hour.

3. Heat oven to 375 degrees. Cut dough in half; keep one half refrigerated. Shape into 1-inch balls. Place 2 inches apart on an ungreased cookie sheet. Flatten to ¼-inch thickness with the bottom of a flour-coated glass.

4. Bake cookies until edges are lightly brown, 7 to 9 minutes. Cool on cookie sheet 1 minute. Transfer to a cooling rack. Repeat process with remaining dough. When completely cooled, place in freezer; chill 15 minutes.

5. Melt chocolates together. Dip half of each cookie in chocolate; shake off excess. Place on cookie sheets lined with wax paper. Place in freezer 10 minutes to set chocolate.

CHOCOLATE DELIGHTS

CHOCOLATE DELIGHTS

Chocolate Crowns (opposite)

Chocolate Crowns

Jacqueline Durkin developed this 2003 honorable mention recipe as a way to replace a store-bought cookie that is no longer produced. Durkin said her family of "superb" cooks didn't allow her to buy cookies from the store, but she loved certain crown-shaped ones made by Nabisco. Her tribute to that cookie features nuts, raspberry jam and marshmallow crowning a chocolate pastry.

Dough:

1½	cups flour
⅓	cup cocoa
1	teaspoon baking soda
¼	teaspoon salt
1	cup packed light brown sugar
1	stick (½ cup) unsalted butter
1	egg
1	teaspoon vanilla extract
½	cup sour cream
1	cup chopped pecans
1	jar (12 ounces) raspberry jam
30	large marshmallows, halved

Icing:

1	cup semisweet chocolate pieces
⅓	cup evaporated milk
1	teaspoon butter
1	teaspoon vanilla extract
½	cup confectioners' sugar

Prep time: 45 minutes

Bake time: 10 minutes per batch

1. Heat oven to 350 degrees. Sift together flour, cocoa, baking soda and salt into medium bowl; set aside. Beat together brown sugar and butter in bowl of electric mixer on medium speed until light and fluffy, about 3 minutes. Beat in egg and vanilla. Reduce speed to low. Alternately beat in one-third of the flour mixture and the sour cream, beating until smooth after each addition. Stir in pecans. Drop by teaspoon onto greased cookie sheet. Bake until slightly brown around the edges, about 10 minutes.

2. Make an indentation in the center of the warm cookies with the back of a spoon; fill with about ¼ teaspoon of the jam. Top with marshmallow, cut-side down. Return cookies to oven until marshmallow melts slightly, about 30 seconds. Transfer to wire racks; cool.

3. Meanwhile, for icing, melt chocolate pieces in a double boiler over simmering water. Stir in milk, butter and vanilla. Stir in confectioners' sugar. Remove from heat; beat until mixture can be spread. Spoon icing over marshmallows; spread with a knife to cover marshmallows completely.

Chocolate Almond Shortbread

This recipe, submitted by Betty Koenig, won second place in 2012. She adapted it from a shortbread recipe, and although the shape of these cookies might bring a different holiday to mind, Koenig said she sees them tied to Christmas. "The essential part of Christmas is love," she wrote. "The heart of Christmas is just that."

Yield: 4 dozen cookies

4 sticks (1 pound) unsalted butter, softened

1 cup sugar

1½ teaspoons vanilla

½ teaspoon salt

3 cups flour

1 cup Dutch process unsweetened cocoa powder, see note on p. 198

1 cup almond meal or very finely ground unblanched almonds

Prep time: 45 minutes

Chill time: 30 minutes

Bake time: 20 minutes per batch

1. Heat oven to 325 degrees. Cream butter and sugar in a large bowl with an electric mixer or in a stand mixer. Add the vanilla and salt; beat or mix to blend. On low speed, add the flour, cocoa and almond meal, mixing well.

2. Divide into 3 pieces; wrap in plastic wrap and chill, 30 minutes. Roll out dough, one piece at a time, on a lightly floured surface to about ¼-inch thickness. Cut with cookie cutters; transfer to parchment-lined cookie sheet. Repeat with remaining dough.

3. Bake, in batches if necessary, until slightly firm to the touch, about 20 minutes. Cool on racks. Store in airtight containers. Can be frozen for months.

Clockwise from top left: Grandma Hazucha's Kolacky (p. 80); Lime Pistachio Cookies (p. 92); Middle East Fruit Bars (p. 95); Chocolate Almond Shortbread (opposite); H-Bars (p. 197)

From top: Pecan Tassies
(p. 100); Chocolate Mint
Sticks (opposite)

Yield: About 3 dozen bars

Chocolate Mint Sticks

Jill Kaltenhaler's third-place recipe from the 1992 contest is a chocolate lover's dream. The fudgy cookies, a favorite of Kaltenhaler's husband, are topped with green mint and chocolate frosting. For holiday cookie trays, cut the brownies into small squares and decorate them with holiday finery.

Batter:

1	cup (2 sticks) butter or margarine, softened
2	cups granulated sugar
4	large eggs
2	teaspoons vanilla
4	ounces unsweetened chocolate, melted
1	cup unsifted all-purpose flour
¾	cup chopped pecans or walnuts

Mint filling:

2	cups confectioners' sugar
4	tablespoons butter or margarine, softened
2	tablespoons milk
½	teaspoon peppermint extract
1-2	drops green food coloring, if desired

Glaze:

2	ounces unsweetened chocolate
2	tablespoons butter or margarine

Prep time: 25 minutes

Bake time: 30 minutes per batch

1. Heat oven to 350 degrees. Grease a 13-by-9-inch baking pan.

2. With an electric mixer, cream the butter, granulated sugar, eggs and vanilla until light, 2 minutes. Add the chocolate and mix well. Stop the mixer and fold in the flour, then the nuts.

3. Transfer batter to prepared pan. Bake just until a toothpick inserted in the center comes out clean, 30 minutes. Cool completely.

4. For the filling, mix all ingredients until smooth. Spread in an even layer over the cooled brownies.

5. For the glaze, melt chocolate with butter; mix well. Pour over filling and gently tilt pan so glaze covers the entire surface. Refrigerate until glaze is set; cut into squares or sticks.

Yield: About 2 dozen brownies

¾ cup all-purpose flour

¼ teaspoon baking powder

¼ teaspoon salt

½ cup (1 stick) unsalted butter

3 ounces unsweetened baking chocolate

1 cup sugar

1 teaspoon vanilla extract

2 large eggs, room temperature

½ cup semisweet chocolate chips

Prep time: 20 minutes

Bake time: 20 to 25 minutes per batch

Fudgy Bittersweet Brownie Stars

These third-place winners in 1997 came from Jean Cummings, who earned the title of the "Cummings cookie elf" for her December baking marathons. One year, she used 25 pounds of butter for cookies alone.

1. Heat oven to 350 degrees. Line bottom and sides of a 13-by-9-inch pan with foil, leaving 2-inch overhang at each end. Butter the foil, including sides and bottom; set aside.

2. Sift together flour, baking powder and salt; set aside. Melt butter in 3-quart pan over medium heat. Add unsweetened chocolate; stir until melted. Remove from heat. Stir in sugar and vanilla; mix well. Stir in eggs, mixing well. Stir in flour mixture and chocolate chips.

3. Spread batter evenly in prepared pan. Bake 20 to 25 minutes, until tops of brownies are firm when gently touched. Cool completely on wire rack; lift foil and brownies from pan. Cut brownies with 2-inch star-shaped cookie cutter (or your favorite cutter). Decorate with colored sugar, sprinkles or frosting, as desired.

German Chocolate Coffee Pretzels

Dough:

1¾ cups flour

⅓ cup plus 1 tablespoon unsweetened dark cocoa powder

½ teaspoon cinnamon

¼ teaspoon plus ⅛ teaspoon salt

1½ sticks (¾ cup) plus 2 tablespoons butter, softened

1 cup granulated sugar

2 teaspoons instant coffee powder, see note

1 egg

1 teaspoon coffee-flavored liqueur

Topping:

1 egg white beaten with 2 teaspoons water for glaze

⅓ cup vanilla sugar, see note, or sanding sugar

4 ounces bittersweet chocolate, melted, see note

Prep time: 1 hour

Chill time: 30 minutes

Bake time: 8 to 11 minutes per batch

Rest time: 5 to 15 minutes

1. For the dough, stir flour, cocoa, cinnamon and salt together in a bowl; set aside.

2. Beat butter, sugar and coffee together in another bowl until light and fluffy. Blend in egg and coffee liqueur. Stir in flour mixture ½ cup at a time, blending well after each addition. Form dough into a log 11 inches long and 2 inches in diameter. Wrap log in wax paper. Place wrapped dough in a plastic freezer bag. Freeze until firm, about 30 minutes.

3. Heat oven to 350 degrees. Line 3 large baking sheets with parchment paper. On a lightly floured surface, cut chilled dough into ⅜-inch-thick slices. Work with a few slices at once, keeping the remainder refrigerated so that they remain cold. Using your palms, roll each slice back and forth into a rope about 14 inches long and ¼ inch in diameter.

4. Shape each rope into a pretzel: Cross one end over the other, creating a center loop at top and leaving ends 2 to 2½ inches on each side. Twist ends at crossed intersection once. Flip ends toward the top loop. Press each end into center loop dough section about 1½ inches apart.

5. Use a spatula to transfer pretzels to a cutting board. For the topping, brush pretzels with egg glaze then sprinkle with vanilla sugar. (This step is not done on the baking sheet because the egg and sugar will cause the pretzels to stick.) Transfer sugared pretzels to parchment-lined baking sheet. Bake until firm to the touch, 8 to 11 minutes. Cool on racks.

6. Drizzle melted chocolate on top of cooled pretzels. Allow chocolate drizzle to harden, 5 to 15 minutes. Store in an airtight container at room temperature 1 week. Freeze for longer storage. Dough may be made and frozen up to 2 weeks in advance.

Cassandra Wiese found this recipe in her high school library after her German teacher assigned the class to make an authentic German dish. She has since adapted it to her family's particular tastes. These pretzels, which Wiese said pair delightfully with Kahlúa, won second place in 2013.

Note: If the instant coffee is in granular form, mash the granules into a powder with the back of a spoon. To make vanilla sugar, place a vanilla bean in a container of sugar, 1 or 2 weeks.

Melting chocolate: Melt chocolate in a heatproof bowl over a saucepan of simmering water, stirring occasionally. If using a microwave, place chopped chocolate squares or chips in a microwave-safe bowl. Microwave on 50 percent power, 1 minute. Stir. Continue microwaving at 30-second intervals on medium power, stirring after each interval, until chocolate is smooth.

Yield: 30 to 36 cookies

Pictured on p. 19

Dough:

1 cup (2 sticks) unsalted butter, softened

2¼ cups all-purpose flour

⅓ cup confectioners' sugar, sifted

1 teaspoon pure vanilla extract

1 teaspoon water

About 36 thin layered chocolate mint wafers (or other flavor miniature chocolates), unwrapped

Icing:

Confectioners' sugar

Milk

Food coloring as desired

Colored sprinkles as desired

Prep time: 2 hours

Bake time: 15 to 20 minutes per batch

Surprise Packages

These 1994 second-place winners from Carol Feezell can be made with several kinds of miniature candies. She suggested filling them with chocolate mint wafers, such as Andes, or Hershey's Miniatures. Feezell said these cookies are a symbol of Christmas for her, as their "delicate butter, mint and chocolate flavor elicit feelings of Christmas with the first taste."

1. Heat oven to 325 degrees. Have ready ungreased baking sheets.

2. Beat butter in large bowl of electric mixer until light and fluffy. Beat in half of the flour, the sugar, vanilla and water until thoroughly combined. Beat in the remaining flour.

3. Use a scant 1 tablespoon of dough and press it flat and thin with your hands. Put a chocolate mint wafer in the center and fold the dough over to completely cover each chocolate and to form a neat, rectangular package. Pinch the edges to seal. Place 1 inch apart on ungreased baking sheets.

4. Bake until bottoms are lightly browned, 15 to 20 minutes. Cool a few minutes on the baking sheets and then cool completely on wire racks.

5. For icing, mix confectioners' sugar and milk to make a thin icing; color icing as desired. Use a small spatula to ice cookies. Decorate as desired so cookies resemble Christmas packages.

Yield: 10½ dozen cookies

Chocolate Zingers

These petite and crispy chocolate cookies came from Elaine Rysner, who earned an honorable mention in the 2006 contest. Rysner said her staple ingredients are always well stocked so she can try any new recipe on a whim.

3	cups flour
1½	cups unsweetened cocoa powder
1	teaspoon cinnamon
½	teaspoon black pepper
½	teaspoon red pepper
¼	teaspoon salt
1¾	cups sugar
3	sticks (1½ cups) unsalted butter
2	eggs, lightly beaten

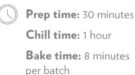

Prep time: 30 minutes

Chill time: 1 hour

Bake time: 8 minutes per batch

1. Sift together the flour, cocoa, cinnamon, peppers and salt in a large bowl; set aside. Beat sugar and butter in a medium bowl until creamy with a mixer on medium speed. Add eggs, beating in one at a time, until fluffy. Stir in the flour mixture until just combined. Divide dough into 3 parts; wrap each in plastic wrap. Refrigerate 1 hour.

2. Heat oven to 375 degrees. Roll dough in batches to ⅛-inch thickness on a floured work surface. Cut into star shapes. Transfer to a greased or parchment-covered baking sheet. Bake until cookies are firm, about 8 minutes.

Emily Dugan brought these cookies on one of her first dates
with her husband, a caterer/personal chef. "He told me he's not
a sweets guy, but **he definitely ate more than one,**" she
recalled. The cookies won second place in the 2010 contest.

Yield: 3 dozen cookies

Emily Dugan's Triple-Chocolate Walnut Cookies

2¼ cups flour

½ cup cocoa

1 teaspoon baking soda

½ teaspoon salt

2 sticks (1 cup) butter, softened

1 cup firmly packed brown sugar

¾ cup granulated sugar

2 eggs

1 teaspoon chocolate extract

1 bag (12 ounces) semisweet chocolate chips

1½ cups chopped walnuts

Prep time: 25 minutes

Bake time: 11 to 14 minutes per batch

1. Heat oven to 375 degrees. Stir together flour, cocoa, baking soda and salt in a medium bowl; set aside. Mix butter and sugars by hand or with mixer in a large bowl until light and fluffy. Mix in eggs one at a time. Mix in chocolate extract. Add half of the flour mixture to butter mixture; mix to combine. Mix in remaining flour. Stir in chocolate chips and walnuts.

2. Scoop dough with a small ice-cream scoop or tablespoon onto silicone mat- or parchment-lined cookie sheets. Bake until lightly browned on bottom, 11 to 14 minutes. Let cool 2 minutes on cookie sheet; transfer to a wire rack. Cool completely.

Crispy Chocolate Jumbles

Michael Reinhart pieced together this cookie recipe from an ingredient list he found among some papers he inherited from his grandmother after she died. Without any measurements or directions, Reinhart had to re-create his favorite childhood recipe through trial and error. After a dozen attempts, he finally got it right and won third place in the 2007 contest.

1¼ cups flour
 ½ teaspoon baking soda
 ⅛ teaspoon salt
 1 stick (½ cup) butter, softened
 1 cup sugar
 1 egg
 1 teaspoon vanilla
 2 cups crisp rice cereal
 2 cups semisweet chocolate chips
 ½ cup dried chopped cranberries or cherries

Prep time: 25 minutes

Bake time: 10 to 12 minutes per batch

1. Heat oven to 350 degrees. Sift together the flour, baking soda and salt in a medium bowl; set aside.

2. Beat the butter and sugar together in a large bowl with a mixer on medium speed until creamy, about 3 minutes. Beat in the egg and vanilla until light and fluffy, about 3 minutes. Stir in the reserved flour mixture; stir in the cereal, chocolate chips and dried cranberries just until mixed.

3. Drop tablespoonfuls on a lightly greased baking sheet; bake until golden, about 10 to 12 minutes. Transfer to a wire rack to cool.

Colleen Frankhart used Dorie Greenspan's recipe to get her through a romantic rough spot. **"We fought. We cried. We ate cookies. We made up. We ate more cookies,"** she wrote in the essay accompanying these impeccable chocolate icebox cookies. Frankhart won second place in the 2008 contest for this recipe.

Yield: 3 dozen cookies

1¼ cups flour
⅓ cup Dutch process cocoa powder, see note on p. 198
½ teaspoon baking soda
1 stick plus 3 tablespoons unsalted butter, room temperature
⅔ cup packed light brown sugar
¼ cup granulated sugar
1 teaspoon vanilla
½ teaspoon sea salt
5 ounces bittersweet chocolate, chopped into small bits

Prep time: 25 minutes

Chill time: 1 hour

Bake time: 14 minutes per batch

Dorie's Dark and Stormies

1. Sift the flour, cocoa and baking soda together in small bowl; set aside. Beat the butter until smooth in bowl of an electric mixer at medium speed. Add the sugars, vanilla and salt; beat 2 minutes. Reduce speed to low; add the flour mixture, mixing until incorporated but still crumbly, and being careful not to overwork the dough. Stir in the chocolate pieces.

2. Turn the dough out onto a smooth work surface; squeeze it so that it sticks together in large clumps. (If you need to, it's OK to lightly flour the work surface.) Gather the dough into a ball; divide in half. Shape each ball into a log 1½ inches in diameter. Wrap logs in plastic wrap; chill at least 1 hour.

3. Heat oven to 325 degrees. Line two baking sheets with parchment. Gently slice logs into ½-inch rounds using a serrated knife (some will crumble; simply press broken bits back onto cookie). Place 1 inch apart on the baking sheets.

4. Bake, one sheet at a time, 14 minutes; cookies will not look done or be firm. Cool on pan 5 minutes; transfer to cooling rack. Cool to room temperature.

Note: Dough can be made ahead and frozen. Frozen dough doesn't need to be defrosted before baking; just slice logs and bake 1 minute longer. Packed airtight, cookies will keep at room temperature up to 3 days or frozen up to a month.

Babs Bufton's Chocolate Melting Moments

1 stick (½ cup) butter, softened

½ cup confectioners' sugar, sifted

1 cup flour

1 tablespoon unsweetened cocoa

3½ ounces (about ½ cup) semisweet chocolate, melted, cooled

Prep time: 30 minutes

Bake time: 15 minutes per batch

1. Heat oven to 350 degrees. Beat butter and sugar together in large bowl with mixer until light and fluffy. Sift flour and cocoa into the bowl; beat just until smooth enough to pipe.

2. Spoon mixture into a large piping bag with a ¾-inch fluted round tip. Pipe out 3-inch lengths onto a greased or parchment-lined cookie sheet, allowing space between for expansion.

3. Bake until firm when lightly pressed, 15 minutes. Let cool slightly on sheet; transfer to a wire rack to cool. Dip both ends of the cooled cookies into the melted chocolate; let set on wire rack.

This recipe came from Babs Bufton, a born-and-bred Brit who followed her husband's job transfer to Illinois. It won third place in the 2010 contest. Bufton recommended using a metal fluted tip on a pastry bag to form these cookies because the ridges will be sharper. You could also use a cookie press.

Black-Out Cookies

2 squares (1 ounce each) unsweetened chocolate

2 eggs, beaten

1 cup sugar

¼ cup vegetable oil

1 teaspoon vanilla extract

1 teaspoon chocolate extract

1 cup flour

¾ teaspoon baking powder

¼ teaspoon salt

½ cup confectioners' sugar

Prep time: 30 minutes

Chill time: 3 hours

Bake time: 10 minutes per batch

1. Melt the chocolate in the top of a double boiler set over simmering water; set aside to cool slightly. Combine eggs, sugar, oil and extracts in a large bowl; whisk to combine. Stir in the chocolate; set aside.

2. Whisk together the flour, baking powder and salt in a large bowl. Add chocolate mixture to flour mixture, stirring until well combined. Cover; refrigerate at least 3 hours.

3. Heat oven to 350 degrees. Spread confectioners' sugar on a plate; set aside. Scoop walnut-size balls of dough; roll each in the sugar. Place on a greased or parchment-lined cookie sheet 2 inches apart. Bake until edges are firm, about 10 minutes per batch. Remove cookies to a wire rack; cool.

A very soft dough bakes into a rich chocolate cookie in this recipe from Shana Schuman and her daughter Zehava, who won first place in 2006. Zehava named the sugar-dusted chocolate pastries "black-out cookies" because they were inspired by a blackout caused by a snowstorm.

Yield: 52 cookies

Sylvia's Coo Coo Cookies

These cookies came from Susan Stone, who earned an honorable mention in the 2010 competition, and are named for her late mother, Sylvia.

Dough:

1¾ cups sifted flour

½ cup Dutch process unsweetened cocoa powder, see note on p. 198

½ teaspoon baking soda

1 stick (½ cup) butter, room temperature

1 cup sugar

1 egg

1 teaspoon vanilla

½ cup milk

½ cup chopped walnuts

26 marshmallows, cut in half

Chocolate glaze and topping:

1½ cups confectioners' sugar

½ cup Dutch process unsweetened cocoa powder

3–4 tablespoons hot water

⅓ cup melted butter

Prep time: 25 minutes

Bake time: 11 minutes per batch

1. Heat oven to 375 degrees. Sift flour, cocoa powder and baking soda together in medium bowl; set aside. Cream butter in a large bowl with a mixer until light and fluffy, 2 minutes. Add sugar; beat until pale. Beat in egg until smooth, 2 minutes. Beat in vanilla. Beat in flour mixture in batches alternately with the milk. Beat until smooth. Stir in nuts.

2. Drop teaspoonfuls on a parchment-lined cookie sheet. Bake 9 minutes. Remove cookies from oven; press ½ of a marshmallow into the center of each cookie. Bake 2 minutes. Remove from oven.

3. Meanwhile, for glaze, sift confectioners' sugar and cocoa powder together in a medium bowl. Whisk in 3 tablespoons of the hot water. Whisk in the melted butter until smooth. Add more hot water if necessary to make a smooth glaze. Immediately spoon/drizzle the chocolate glaze over each cookie. Transfer to wire rack to cool.

Yield: About 3 dozen cookies

Chocolate Shots

Kimberly H. McGuire of Oak Park took top honors in 1996 with her dual win: a lovely story of her grandmother and the keeping of tradition, and her delicious cookie, crisp with oatmeal and butter and ringed with chocolate. In her letter, she wrote, "My grandmother was the family baker. She was forever baking delicacies appropriate to each season in great abundance... In many ways it was her greatest joy to share her treats with us each year." No less an authority than Julia Child, who was a guest judge during a visit to Chicago, rated the cookie an 8 out of 9 points: "I liked the crisp crunch of it; it was a very nice cookie," she said, after taking tiny bites of each of the 15 finalists' cookies. The other judges concurred. They liked McGuire's cookie for its "light texture" and its "buttery flavor." Judges included five members of the Good Eating staff and pastry chef Gale Gand.

1 cup (2 sticks) unsalted butter, softened

1 cup confectioners' sugar

2 tablespoons vanilla extract

1½ cups all-purpose flour

½ teaspoon baking soda

1 cup rolled oats, not instant

3 bottles (1.75 ounces each) chocolate sprinkles

Prep time: 15 minutes

Chill time: 10 minutes plus overnight

Bake time: 20 minutes per batch

1. Beat butter in large bowl of electric mixer at high speed until creamy, about 1 minute. Add sugar and vanilla; beat until light and fluffy, about 2 minutes. Gradually beat in flour and baking soda until smooth. Stir in oats. Refrigerate dough in mixer bowl 10 minutes for easier handling.

2. Remove dough from refrigerator. Divide dough into 2 to 3 equal pieces. Roll each piece into a log about 1½ inches in diameter. Pour sprinkles into pie plate; roll logs in sprinkles to coat evenly. Wrap logs in plastic wrap and refrigerate overnight.

3. Heat oven to 325 degrees. Cut dough into ¼-inch slices. Bake on greased baking sheet until lightly browned and slightly firm to the touch, about 20 minutes. Remove to cooling rack.

SANDWICH COOKIES

SANDWICH COOKIES

Laced Cookies

Apricot Marzipan Hearts

Maria Damp was awarded an honorable mention in the 2009 contest for this recipe, which was adapted from "Weihnachtsbackerei von Anisplatzchen bis Zimtstern" by Gisela Allkemper.

½ cup softened butter

½ cup sugar

1 egg

1 cup marzipan paste

1 cup flour, plus more for rolling

1 cup finely chopped roasted, unsalted almonds

¼ cup dried apricots, finely chopped

Finely grated zest of 1 lemon

1 cup apricot jam, melted

Confectioners' sugar, optional

Prep time: 1 hour

Chill time: 30 minutes

Bake time: 8 to 10 minutes per batch

1. Combine butter and sugar in large bowl; beat until fluffy with electric mixer. Beat in egg until smooth. Beat in marzipan paste. Stir in flour until incorporated. Stir in almonds, apricots and lemon zest. Chill dough at least 30 minutes.

2. Heat oven to 350 degrees. Roll out dough to about ⅛-inch thickness on lightly floured board (dough will be very sticky). Cut into shapes with a floured heart-shaped or other cookie cutter. Place hearts on parchment-lined cookie sheets. Bake until lightly golden, 8 to 10 minutes per batch. Transfer to wire racks to cool.

3. Spread a thin layer of jam on one cookie; top with another cookie. Repeat with remaining cookies. Sift confectioners' sugar over tops.

Brown Butter Maple Spritz

Sarah Frudden's Wisconsin dairyland heritage clearly shines through in this indulgent ode to butter. The recipe, which won second place in 1995, was based on an old family favorite that Frudden updated with maple syrup and a rich, buttery filling. She said the flavors in these cookies remind her of winter in Wisconsin.

1¼ cups (2½ sticks) unsalted butter

1 cup confectioners' sugar

2 teaspoons pure vanilla extract

1¼ teaspoon salt

1 large egg

2 large egg yolks

2¼ cups unsifted all-purpose flour

½ cup pure maple syrup

Milk or whipping cream, if necessary

🕐 **Prep time:** 1 hour

Chill time: 30 minutes or longer

Bake time: 16 to 18 minutes per batch

1. To brown the butter, melt in a small, heavy saucepan over low heat. When fully melted, increase heat to medium and cook, stirring constantly, until the butter turns a medium brown and smells nutty. Measure out 1 cup to use for cookies, and reserve the rest for the filling. Refrigerate until firm but not solid, about 30 minutes.

2. For cookies, heat oven to 325 degrees. Have ready a cookie press and ungreased baking sheet(s).

3. Beat the 1 cup brown butter, ½ cup of the confectioners' sugar, vanilla and salt in large bowl of electric mixer until creamy. Add egg and egg yolks and mix to combine. Stop mixer and add flour; mix on low speed just until flour disappears.

4. Transfer dough to a cookie press and press onto baking sheet in desired shapes, spacing them 1½ inches apart. Bake until set, 16 to 18 minutes. Transfer to a wire rack to cool.

5. For filling, cook maple syrup in a heavy 2-quart saucepan over high heat for 5 minutes. Cool to lukewarm then stir in remaining ½ cup confectioners' sugar. Beat the reserved brown butter in a food processor or a small bowl of electric mixer until light. Add the syrup mixture and beat until smooth. If mixture is too thick, add a small amount of milk or cream until it is spreadable.

6. Assemble cookies by spreading about ½ teaspoon filling on the flat side of half the cookies. Sandwich with another cookie.

Yield: 3 dozen sandwich cookies

3 cups flour, plus more for dusting

⅔ cup granulated sugar

1 teaspoon baking powder

2½ sticks (1¼ cups) butter or margarine, softened, cut into pieces

4 egg yolks, lightly beaten

1–2 teaspoons sour cream, if necessary

1 cup confectioners' sugar

1 teaspoon vanilla sugar, optional, see note

1 jar apricot jelly, see note

Prep time: 30 minutes

Chill time: 1 hour

Bake time: 12 minutes per batch

Cool time: 10 minutes

The Family Jewels

1. Mound flour, granulated sugar and baking powder on a wooden board. Work the butter into the dry ingredients by hand until dough forms. Make a well in center of mound; add the egg yolks. Combine by hand, kneading dough until ingredients are thoroughly blended. If resulting dough will not form a ball, add 1 teaspoon sour cream; continue kneading. Add remaining sour cream if needed. Chill dough at least 1 hour.

2. Heat oven to 350 degrees. Scrape board; dust with flour. Divide dough in half; roll each half to ¼-inch thickness. Cut out cookies using 3-inch scalloped cookie cutter; cut round center hole (½ to 1 inch) in half of the cookies. (We used the lid of an olive oil jar.) Reroll scraps and continue cutting out more cookies.

3. Bake on lightly greased baking sheet until golden, about 12 minutes; let cool 10 minutes on pan and finish cooling on wire rack. Mix together confectioners' sugar and vanilla sugar; dust cookie tops (with center holes) with mixture.

4. Spread the softened jelly on cookie bottoms (no holes); place tops over filled bottoms, allowing filling to swell in center. Store overnight in tin container to allow jelly to moisten and set cookies.

Note: To soften jelly, microwave the opened jar about 30 seconds on high. Vanilla sugar is sold in some specialty markets, but it's easy to make. The week before you need it, place 1 vanilla bean in 1 pound sugar. It can be stored in an airtight container for up to 6 months.

These pretty morsels come from Marissa Hegel, who won an honorable mention in the 2008 contest. **"I have been baking Christmas cookies since I was 3 years old,"** she wrote in her essay. "In the weeks between Thanksgiving and Christmas, my grandmother, my mother, my sister and I would work as a team, churning out the dozens of cookies that would grace our holiday dessert tables."

Yield: 40 sandwich cookies

Hazelnut Espresso Truffle Cookies

This fragrant concoction from Cindy Beberman blends chocolate, espresso and roasted hazelnuts. Beberman won first place in 2005 for this recipe, which she described as producing "a uniquely rich, grown-up version of a rolled cutout cookie." Her recipe is based on her sister's enthusiastic description of a hazelnut cookie sampled during a vacation in Liguria.

Dough:

1½	cups shelled hazelnuts
2½	cups flour
¼	teaspoon baking powder
1¼	cups superfine sugar, see note
2	sticks (1 cup) unsalted butter, softened
½	teaspoon salt
1	egg
1	egg yolk
2	teaspoons vanilla
1	tablespoon plus 1 teaspoon instant espresso powder

Truffle filling:

1	container (½ pint) whipping cream
9	ounces milk chocolate, finely chopped
5	ounces semisweet chocolate, finely chopped

Decorating trim:

8	ounces semisweet chocolate chips

1. Heat oven to 350 degrees. Place hazelnuts on a baking sheet; roast until golden brown, about 14 minutes. Remove from oven; rub briskly in a clean towel while still warm to remove most of the skins. Let cool completely. Finely chop nuts; set aside. Sift the flour and baking powder together in a medium bowl; set aside.

2. Beat the sugar, butter and salt in large bowl with a mixer on medium-high speed until light and fluffy, about 3 minutes. Beat in whole egg, egg yolk and vanilla until mixed; beat in espresso powder until mixed. Reduce mixer speed to low; beat in reserved nuts.

3. Beat reserved flour mixture into batter until just mixed. Divide dough in half; shape into 2 discs. Wrap each disc in plastic wrap; refrigerate until firm, about 1 hour.

4. Meanwhile, for truffle filling, heat the cream in a small saucepan over medium heat just to a boil; remove from heat. Place chopped chocolate in a medium bowl; add cream, stirring until chocolate melts and mixture is smooth. Refrigerate, uncovered, occasionally stirring, until chocolate thickens and is spreadable, about 45 minutes.

5. Heat oven to 375 degrees. Divide one disc in half; return 1½ discs to refrigerator. Roll out the half-disc on a lightly floured board to ⅛-inch thickness. Cut into trees or other shapes with cookie cutter; place cookies

Prep time: 2 hours

Chill time: 1 hour

Bake time: 7 to 8 minutes per batch

Freeze time: 10 minutes

½ inch apart on parchment-lined baking sheet. Bake until edges just begin to brown, about 7 to 8 minutes. Cool on sheet 1 minute; transfer cookies to wire rack to cool completely. Repeat with remaining dough.

6. Spread truffle filling on the bottom of 1 cookie; place a second cookie on top of the filling, sandwich style. Place filled cookies on wire rack to cool. Repeat with remaining cookies. (If chocolate thickens too much before cookies are filled, set the bowl in a larger bowl of hot water and stir to soften.)

7. For decoration, heat chocolate chips in a saucepan over very low heat, stirring constantly; spoon into a pastry bag fitted with a fine writing tip. Pipe thin lines of chocolate back and forth over the top of each cookie; place sheets of cookies in freezer until chocolate sets, about 10 minutes. Store cookies in airtight containers in refrigerator, 5 to 7 days, or freeze up to 3 months.

Note: Superfine sugar is sold in supermarket baking sections; you also can process regular sugar in a food processor for 30 seconds.

Yield: About 3 dozen
sandwich cookies

5 cups all-purpose flour
1 cup sugar
2 cups (4 sticks) cold butter
4 large egg yolks
2 large eggs
1 tablespoon vanilla
   extract
   Decorative sprinkles
½ cup your favorite
   flavored jam

Prep time: 45 minutes

Bake time: 7 to 9 minutes
per batch

Jam-Filled Butter Cookies

Caroline St. Clair tied for third place in 1998 with
these festive and buttery treats. She said these cookies
evoke memories of her late grandmother, who "had so
much patience and love for baking that she probably
had given a name to each and every cookie she made."

1. Heat oven to 350 degrees. Stir together flour and
sugar in large bowl. Cut butter into flour mixture using
pastry blender or two knives until size of very small
peas. Add egg yolks, 1 of the whole eggs and vanilla;
stir well.

2. Roll out dough in batches on lightly floured surface
to ⅛-inch thickness. Cut out dough with 2-inch cookie
cutter. Cut ½-inch circle from center of half the cookies using end of small pastry tip or thimble to make
cookie tops. Place tops and bottoms on lightly greased
baking sheet. Lightly beat remaining egg. Brush over
cookie tops; decorate tops with sprinkles.

3. Bake cookies until set and glaze is slightly golden,
7 to 9 minutes. Cool completely on wire rack. Place
½ teaspoon jam in center of bottom cookies; spread
slightly. Place top cookies over each bottom; press
down lightly.

Yield: 1½ dozen sandwich cookies

Jelly Christmas Eyes

Mary Vodisek received an honorable mention in 1989 for this recipe. She said her mother, who was politically involved against the Communists in her homeland of Yugoslavia, packed a copy of her own mother's recipes with her when she was forced to flee the country. She realized "these would provide the fondest memories of her childhood and homeland," Vodisek wrote.

½ cup (1 stick) margarine
⅓ cup sugar
1 large egg
 Juice of 1 lemon
¼ teaspoon grated lemon rind
1⅓ cups all-purpose flour
½ cup ground almonds or walnuts
 Raspberry or strawberry jelly
 Granulated sugar, for coating

Prep time: 20 minutes

Chill time: 30 minutes

Bake time: 10 to 12 minutes per batch

1. Cream margarine and sugar in mixing bowl. Add egg, lemon juice and lemon rind. Mix until smooth. Add flour and nuts. Wrap in plastic wrap and flatten. Refrigerate dough 30 minutes.

2. Heat oven to 350 degrees. Roll out dough on lightly floured surface to ⅛-inch thickness. Use a round 2-inch cookie cutter to cut out circles from dough. Cut out an inner circle with a smaller round cookie cutter from half of the circles to make a "cookie ring."

3. Bake circles and rings until light golden, 10 to 12 minutes. Transfer to wire rack to cool. Spread a small amount of jelly on each whole circle. Press a cookie ring on top of it. Shake the cookies one at a time in a bowl of sugar to coat well. Store in a covered dish.

Note: Confectioners' sugar can be used to coat the cookies in place of granulated.

Yield: 3 dozen sandwich cookies

1 cup (2 sticks) unsalted butter, softened

1¾ cups confectioners' sugar

1½ teaspoons pure vanilla extract

1½ cups all-purpose flour, sifted before measuring

½ cup finely ground hazelnuts or macadamia nuts

About ¼ cup seedless raspberry preserves

Food coloring as desired, for decorating

Prep time: 1 hour

Bake time: 9 to 11 minutes per batch

Joan's Little Joys

Isabelle Clarke Garibaldi ranked fifth in the 1995 contest with these nut-flecked butter cookies sandwiched together with fruit preserves.

1. Heat oven to 350 degrees. Lightly grease cookie sheet(s) or line with parchment paper.

2. Beat butter and ½ cup of the confectioners' sugar in large bowl of electric mixer on high speed until well combined. Mix in vanilla. Stop the mixer and add the flour and ground nuts. Mix on low speed just until combined.

3. Using 1 teaspoon dough for each, roll into rounds. Place on baking sheet. Dip the bottom of a flat glass in confectioners' sugar, reserving ¼ cup for this purpose. Press each ball, flattening to a 1-inch round.

4. Bake just until they begin to color, 9 to 11 minutes. Transfer to a wire rack to cool.

5. Spread bottoms of half the cookies with preserves, using about ¼ teaspoon for each cookie. Sandwich together with another cookie.

6. For icing, mix remaining 1 cup confectioners' sugar with just enough water to make it spreading consistency. Tint icing with food coloring, if desired.

7. Decorate top of cookies with icing, using a pastry bag, if desired.

Yield: 3 dozen sandwich cookies

Laced Cookies

Janet Protas' 2001 first-place winners are a variation of lace cookies, a family favorite she said fondly reminds her of her sister, who typed the recipe decades ago on a manual typewriter. Protas uses Valrhona chocolate for the filling of these elegant cookies, but any high-quality baking chocolate will do. Just be sure not to use chocolate chips.

Dough:

2	sticks (1 cup) unsalted butter, room temperature
1	cup granulated sugar
1	cup light brown sugar
2	eggs, room temperature
1	teaspoon almond extract
2½	cups regular or quick cooking oats
1	cup finely chopped walnuts
1	teaspoon baking powder

Filling:

12	ounces semisweet chocolate
4	tablespoons butter
2	tablespoons orange liqueur

Prep time: 1 hour

Bake time: 12 minutes per batch

1. Heat oven to 350 degrees. Place butter and sugars in the bowl of electric mixer; beat until light and soft, about 4 minutes. Add eggs and almond extract; mix until just combined. Mix in oats, walnuts and baking powder on low speed until combined.

2. Drop batter by teaspoonfuls onto parchment or foil-lined cookie sheets, spaced 3 inches apart. Bake until cookies are brown around edges and lighter toward center, about 12 minutes. Let cool on baking sheet set on cooling rack.

3. Melt chocolate and butter in a double boiler over simmering water, stirring frequently, until chocolate and butter are melted and smooth. Remove from heat; stir in orange liqueur.

4. Choose two cooled cookies of the same size. Spread about ¾ teaspoon melted chocolate on bottom side of one cookie, to about ¼ inch from edge. Place bottom of other cookie on top to form a sandwich, pressing lightly to spread filling to edge.

Yield: About 30 two-inch sandwich cookies

Dough:

3 cups all-purpose flour
½ cup granulated sugar
2 large egg yolks, beaten
1 tablespoon pure vanilla extract
½ teaspoon salt
  Grated rind of 1 lemon
1 cup (2 sticks) unsalted butter, softened

Filling:

1 jar (12 ounces) apricot preserves
1 tablespoon fresh lemon juice
1 tablespoon rum
  Confectioners' sugar

Prep time: 1¼ hours

Chill time: 1 hour

Bake time: 10 to 12 minutes per batch

Mozart Cookies

1. Sift flour into a large mixing bowl and make an indentation or well in the center of the flour. Add the sugar, egg yolks, vanilla, salt and lemon rind to the well. Mix the ingredients in the well together with the flour. Cut in the butter using a pastry cutter or two sharp knives. At this point the dough will resemble coarse crumbs. Turn the dough out onto a work surface and knead it with your hands until smooth and firm. Divide dough in half and shape into two balls.

2. Wrap tightly in plastic. Refrigerate until firm enough to roll out, about 1 hour.

3. Meanwhile, heat the apricot preserves over low heat, stirring constantly. Stir in lemon juice and rum. Let cool.

4. Heat oven to 325 degrees. Place the chilled dough on a lightly floured surface or between two sheets of floured wax paper. Roll out with a floured rolling pin to about ¼-inch thickness. Cut out circles of dough about 2 inches in diameter. Place half of the circles onto greased or non-stick cookie sheets. Cut the other half of the circles again with a small shot glass or cookie cutter to form a ring shape. (Make an equal amount of rings to circles.) Place the rings onto buttered baking sheets. Bake until light gold, 10 to 12 minutes. Cool a little on the cookie sheets.

5. To assemble, brush the still-warm circles with the cooled apricot mixture. Place one ring on top of each circle and press gently (they break easily) to secure. Spoon a small dollop of the apricot mixture into the center of the cookies. Sprinkle with confectioners' sugar. Cool. Store in a tightly closed tin.

These buttery rounds infused with bits of lemon and vanilla brought second-place honors to German-born Anne Kroemer in 1993. Kroemer said Mozart cookies were a part of all of her Christmas celebrations in Germany, and her mother and grandmother used to bake batches of them in the weeks prior to the holiday. **She uses a wineglass and a smaller schnapps glass to cut out these cookies,** but round cookie cutters and biscuit cutters work as well.

From top: Mozart Cookies (opposite); Springerle (p. 20)

Pastel Sandwich Cookies

These "adult" cookies from Mary Pisone are flavored with three different liqueurs; you can substitute six teaspoons of one flavor, if you like, or choose your own favorite flavors. Also, you can replace the liqueur with non-alcoholic flavored syrups to make the cookies family-friendly. Pisone earned an honorable mention for this recipe in the 2005 contest.

Dough:

2¼	cups flour
½	teaspoon salt
¼	teaspoon baking powder
2	sticks (1 cup) butter, softened
½	cup confectioners' sugar
2	tablespoons milk
2	teaspoons vanilla

Filling:

2	cups confectioners' sugar
1	stick (½ cup) butter, softened
2	teaspoons vanilla
⅛	teaspoon salt
2	teaspoons raspberry liqueur
2	teaspoons creme de menthe
2	teaspoons chocolate liqueur
	Food coloring, optional

Prep time: 50 minutes

Chill time: 4 hours

Bake time: 10 minutes per batch

1. Sift together the flour, salt and baking powder in a medium bowl; set aside. Beat butter and sugar in a large bowl with a mixer on medium speed until fluffy, about 3 minutes. Add milk and vanilla; beat 2 minutes. Reduce speed to low; add flour mixture in batches, beating after each addition just until mixed. Divide dough in half; wrap each half in wax paper. Refrigerate 4 hours.

2. Heat oven to 350 degrees. Roll half of the chilled dough on a floured surface to ⅛-inch thickness. (Keep remaining dough refrigerated.) Cut into circles with a 1½-inch-round floured biscuit or cookie cutter. Transfer rounds to a lightly greased cookie sheet; pierce with the tines of a fork 4 times. Bake until dough is baked through and firm, about 10 minutes. Remove to wire racks to cool completely. Repeat with remaining dough.

3. For filling, beat sugar, butter, vanilla and salt in a medium bowl with a mixer on low speed; divide mixture among 3 small bowls. Stir in 2 teaspoons of one flavor of liqueur into each bowl; stir in food coloring if desired.

4. Spread 1 heaping teaspoon of filling on bottom of 1 cookie; top with another cookie to make a sandwich. Repeat with remaining cookies. Store in tightly covered container.

Clockwise from top: Raspberry Sandwich
Cookies (opposite); Pecan Dollies (p. 126);
Fresh Fruit Jewels (p. 110)

Yield: 2 dozen sandwich cookies

Raspberry Sandwich Cookies

Jay Crowley won third place in 2002 for these delicate sandwich cookies, which her husband dubbed the "bad-back cookie" because she recruited him to help roll out the dough. When she's pressed for time, Crowley said she makes these cookies without cutting the holes that highlight the raspberry filling.

2 sticks (1 cup) butter or margarine, softened

⅔ cup plus ½ cup granulated sugar

2 eggs, separated

2½ cups flour

¼ teaspoon salt

½ cup ground blanched almonds

Confectioners' sugar

1½ cups raspberry preserves

Prep time: 35 minutes

Chill time: 2 hours

Bake time: 8 to 10 minutes per batch

1. Beat butter in bowl of an electric mixer on medium speed until fluffy; beat in ⅔ cup of the granulated sugar until light and fluffy. Add egg yolks, one at a time, beating well after each addition. Combine flour and salt in small bowl; add to butter mixture. Beat just until dough comes together; divide dough into 2 balls. Cover; chill at least 2 hours. Meanwhile, combine remaining ½ cup of the granulated sugar with the almonds; set aside.

2. Heat oven to 375 degrees. Remove 1 ball of dough from refrigerator. Sift confectioners' sugar lightly over work surface. Roll out dough to ⅛-inch thickness; cut into 2½-inch circles for each sandwich bottom. Roll out remaining ball of chilled dough; cut into rings with 2½-inch doughnut cutter. (Reserve the small centers to bake later, if you wish.)

3. Beat egg whites until frothy. Brush 1 side of the rings and bottoms with egg white; sprinkle with almond mixture. Place almond-side up on lightly greased cookie sheets; bake until light brown, 8 to 10 minutes. Transfer with spatula to wire racks; cool.

4. Dust almond side of cookies with confectioners' sugar. Spread raspberry preserves on non-almond side of bottom cookies; place raspberry side up on platter. Top with rings, almond side up, to make sandwiches.

Yield: About 2 dozen sandwich cookies

Dough:

1   cup vegetable oil
2   sticks (1 cup) butter, softened
1   cup confectioners' sugar
1   cup granulated sugar
2   eggs
1   teaspoon vanilla
4   cups flour
1   teaspoon cream of tartar
1   teaspoon baking soda
1   teaspoon salt
    Granulated sugar, for dipping
¼   cup dark chocolate, melted, for drizzling

Filling:

7   tablespoons butter, softened a bit
1½   cups confectioners' sugar
⅓   cup melted bittersweet chocolate
3   tablespoons beet juice
2   shots of very strong espresso or 1 tablespoon instant coffee granules, ground

Prep time: 60 minutes

Chill time: 1 hour

Bake time: 8 to 10 minutes per batch

Red Velvet Sandwich Cookies

1. Heat oven to 350 degrees. Thoroughly cream the oil, butter and sugars in a bowl with an electric mixer. Add eggs and vanilla; blend together.

2. Sift together flour, cream of tartar, baking soda and salt in a separate bowl; mix into butter mixture. Cover; chill well, about 1 hour.

3. Roll dough into small balls (the diameter of a nickel); dip in granulated sugar. Place on greased or parchment-lined cookie sheets; flatten cookies a bit by pressing down gently with the bottom of a glass tumbler.

4. Bake until very light brown; 8 to 10 minutes. Allow cookies to cool on racks.

5. For filling, cream together butter and sugar with an electric mixer until smooth. Add chocolate, beet juice and coffee.

6. After cookies have cooled completely, spoon filling between two cookies. Continue until all cookies have been filled. Drizzle melted dark chocolate on top of sandwich cookies.

Jane Donaldson won third place in 2013 for this recipe, which she adapted from a friend's sugar cookie recipe. The "red" in these cookies originates from beet juice. "When my children whined, **I told them that Santa was a locavore,**" Donaldson said. She also suggested using more or less coffee or chocolate in the filling to get the color you want.

BROWNIES
& BARS

BROWNIES & BARS

Cranberry-Swirled White Chocolate Cheesecake Bars

Caramel Oat Bars

Karen Kruckenberg earned an honorable mention in the 1996 contest with this simple recipe from England.

Base:

½ cup (1 stick) unsalted butter, softened

¼ cup sugar

¾ cup rolled oats

⅔ cup all-purpose flour

Caramel:

1 can (14 ounces) sweetened condensed milk

½ cup (1 stick) unsalted butter

¼ cup packed brown sugar

1–2 teaspoons vanilla extract

Icing:

¼ cup (½ stick) unsalted butter

2 tablespoons water

2 tablespoons cocoa, sifted

1½ cups confectioners' sugar, sifted

Prep time: 30 minutes

Bake time: 20 minutes per batch

1. Heat oven to 350 degrees. For base, beat butter and sugar in small bowl of electric mixer on medium-high speed until light and fluffy, 3 minutes. Add oats and flour; beat until smooth. Press into greased 8-inch-square or 9-inch-square baking pan. Bake until set, 20 minutes.

2. Meanwhile, prepare caramel mixture. Heat condensed milk, butter and brown sugar to a boil in heavy saucepan over medium heat. Boil, stirring constantly, 5 minutes. Remove from heat; stir in vanilla. Pour caramel mixture over cooked base; allow to cool completely.

3. To prepare icing, melt butter in saucepan over medium heat. Stir in cocoa and water until smooth. Add confectioners' sugar; stir until mixed well. Spread over cooled caramel layer. Allow to set before cutting. Store refrigerated.

Irving Kaplan started baking these cookies when he was 71 but pointed out that mandelbrot is much older. He won third place in the 2008 contest for these cookies, which have **a great crumbly crunch** and a bit more moist chewiness than their close cousin, the biscotti.

Yield: 4 dozen cookies

Irv's Mandelbrot (a.k.a. Biscotti)

3 cups flour

1¼ cups sugar

1 cup chopped almonds

1 cup chopped dried cranberries

2 teaspoons baking powder

⅛ teaspoon salt

3 eggs

1 cup canola oil

1 teaspoon vanilla

Zest of 1 orange

1 teaspoon cinnamon

Prep time: 20 minutes

Bake time: 35 to 45 minutes per batch

1. Heat oven to 325 degrees. Mix together the flour, 1 cup of the sugar, almonds, cranberries, baking powder and salt in a large bowl with electric mixer on low speed; slowly beat in the eggs, oil, vanilla and orange zest.

2. Scrape dough onto a lightly floured wooden board; knead until well mixed. Roll into ball; divide into 4 pieces. Roll each piece into a log about 10 inches long and 3 inches wide. Bake logs, 3 inches apart, on lightly oiled foil-lined cookie sheets until lightly brown and firm, 30 to 40 minutes.

3. Meanwhile, mix together the remaining ¼ cup of the sugar and cinnamon in a small bowl. Remove logs from oven; slide onto cutting board. Let logs cool 5 minutes. Gently cut each log into 12 pieces using a serrated knife. Return cookies, cut side up, to cookie sheet. Sprinkle with sugar-cinnamon mix. Return to oven; bake 5 minutes. Turn off oven; leave cookies overnight to dry out.

Yield: About 4 dozen bars

Pictured on p. 67

Dough:

1   cup (2 sticks) unsalted
    butter, softened

1   cup packed brown sugar

1   large egg

1   teaspoon vanilla

2   tablespoons cinnamon,
    see note

½   teaspoon salt

2   cups all-purpose flour

1   egg white, beaten

Streusel:

6   tablespoons butter, cold

¾   cup all-purpose flour

¾   cup sugar

    Colored sugar for garnish

Prep time: 15 minutes

Bake time: 20 minutes
per batch

Cinnamon Toffee Bars

This recipe placed third in 1989 and came from Mary Pat Knopp, who said she made Christmas cookie baking an educational experience for her brother when she was little. "What a splendid way to learn fractions!" she said.

1. Heat oven to 375 degrees. Grease 15-by-10-inch jellyroll pan. Cream butter, sugar, egg and vanilla in mixing bowl. Stir in cinnamon and salt. Add flour, a little at a time. Blend well. Press into pan to ¼-inch thickness with wax paper.

2. Brush beaten egg white over dough. Combine streusel ingredients in food processor. Process until butter is evenly blended. Sprinkle streusel over dough. Bake 20 minutes. Cool on wire rack 15 minutes. Cut into 2-by-1½-inch bars while still warm.

Note: The test kitchen found that a mixture of spices such as cinnamon, allspice, ginger, cardamom and cloves also works nicely in place of the cinnamon, and for the holiday season, a sprinkling of colored sugar before baking brightens up these cookies.

Yield: 25 bars

Grandma's Christmas Date-Nut Bars

Therese Steinken's chewy, bite-sized bars can be mixed up in one bowl. She got the simple recipe from her grandmother, whom she described as a terrible cook but a fabulous baker. Her grandmother died years ago, so Steinken said she started making these treats every Christmas since then in her memory. They won third prize in 2003.

1	cup sugar
¾	cup flour
¼	teaspoon baking powder
⅛	teaspoon salt
½	cup vegetable oil
2	eggs, beaten
½	teaspoon vanilla extract
1	package (8 ounces) pitted dates, finely chopped
1	cup chopped walnuts
½	cup confectioners' sugar

Prep time: 20 minutes

Bake time: 35 minutes per batch

Cooling time: 15 minutes

1. Heat oven to 350 degrees. Combine sugar, flour, baking powder and salt in a medium bowl. Make a well in the center of flour mixture with a spoon. Add oil, eggs and vanilla extract to the well. Mix ingredients together with a spoon until well blended. Stir in dates and walnuts. Pour into greased 9-inch-square pan.

2. Bake until just golden brown, about 35 minutes. Cool 15 minutes. Cut bars while still warm. Place confectioners' sugar in sieve or strainer; sprinkle sugar on all sides of the bars. Let cool.

Pecan Toasted-Coconut Mandelbrot

This recipe from Evelyn Baumann evolved from one made by Baumann's mother and grandmother. She won first place in the 1998 contest for her mandelbrot, a Jewish cookie very similar to Italian biscotti.

3	cups all-purpose flour
1½	teaspoons baking powder
⅛	teaspoon salt
3	large eggs
1	cup sugar
1	cup vegetable oil
1	teaspoon vanilla
1	teaspoon almond extract
½	teaspoon lemon zest
¾	cup chopped pecans
½	cup unsweetened coconut, toasted

 Prep time: 40 minutes

Chill time: 3 hours

Bake time: 55 minutes per batch

1. Whisk together flour, baking powder and salt in medium bowl; set aside. Beat eggs, sugar and oil in bowl of electric mixer until light in color, about 5 minutes. Beat in extracts and lemon zest. Add ¼ of the flour mixture, pecans and coconut. Mix by hand after each addition until smooth. Wrap dough in plastic wrap; refrigerate at least 3 hours.

2. Heat oven to 350 degrees. Divide dough into 4 equal pieces. Shape dough into 1½-inch-thick logs; place on ungreased baking sheet, about 2 inches apart. Bake until lightly browned, about 25 minutes. Cool on wire rack.

3. Reduce oven to 300 degrees. Slice each log diagonally into ½-inch-thick slices with serrated bread knife. Place back on baking sheet, cut side up. Bake until light golden brown, about 15 minutes; turn each over. Bake 15 more minutes. Cool completely on wire rack.

Yield: 16 bars

Violet Cosimano's Fabulous Walnut Slices

Named after her mother, these cookies by Carole Cosimano received an honorable mention in the 2009 contest.

Dough:

1½	cups brown sugar
½	cup (1 stick) butter
1	cup plus 2 tablespoons flour
2	eggs
1	teaspoon vanilla
½	teaspoon baking powder
¼	teaspoon salt
½	cup shredded coconut
1	cup chopped walnuts

Buttercream frosting:

1	cup sifted confectioners' sugar, plus more for dusting, optional
1–2	tablespoons butter, room temperature
1	teaspoon vanilla
1–2	tablespoons milk

Prep time: 40 minutes

Bake time: 45 minutes per batch

1. Heat oven to 300 degrees. Combine ½ cup of the brown sugar and the butter in a large bowl. Beat with electric mixer until fluffy. Add 1 cup of the flour; beat until crumbly. Pat dough into 8- or 9-inch-square baking pan. Bake 20 minutes. Cool.

2. Increase oven temperature to 350 degrees. Beat eggs in a medium bowl with mixer; beat in remaining 1 cup of the brown sugar. Add vanilla; beat to mix. Mix remaining 2 tablespoons of the flour with baking powder and salt in small bowl; add to egg-brown-sugar mixture. Stir in coconut and walnuts. Spread over prepared pastry. Bake 25 minutes. Cool.

3. Meanwhile, for frosting, combine sugar, butter, vanilla and 1 tablespoon milk in mixing bowl; stir until smooth. Add remaining milk as needed. Cut walnut pastry into squares. Frost squares (or dust with confectioners' sugar).

Victoria Weisenberg won first place in 2012 for this recipe and her tale of using them to **woo "a very special man."** Weisenberg created the recipe as a Hanukkah gift for her former beau and said the "H" stands for the first letter of his first name, though she opted to leave that name a mystery.

Yield: 20 bars

H-Bars

Shortbread:

1 stick (½ cup) unsalted butter, softened

1 cup flour

¼ cup granulated sugar

Raisin layer:

⅓ cup flour

½ teaspoon baking powder

¾ teaspoon cinnamon

¼ teaspoon salt

1 cup brown sugar

2 eggs, lightly beaten

½ teaspoon vanilla

⅔ cup golden raisins

Topping:

½ cup flour

⅓ cup granulated sugar

½ stick (¼ cup) unsalted butter, softened

1 teaspoon cinnamon

Icing:

½ cup confectioners' sugar

1½–2 tablespoons milk

¼ teaspoon vanilla

Prep time: 30 minutes

Bake time: 37 to 40 minutes per batch

1. Grease or coat with cooking spray a 7½-by-11-inch baking pan. Heat oven to 325 degrees.

2. For the shortbread, combine butter, flour and granulated sugar in a medium bowl until crumbly. Pack into the prepared pan; bake, 15 minutes.

3. For raisin layer, stir together flour with the baking powder, cinnamon and salt in a small bowl. In another bowl, beat brown sugar, eggs and vanilla together until blended. Stir in dry ingredients and raisins. Pour over the baked shortbread layer.

4. For the topping, combine ingredients in a bowl until mixture is crumbly. Sprinkle evenly over the raisin layer. Bake, 22 to 25 minutes. Cool.

5. For the icing, combine confectioners' sugar, 1½ tablespoons milk and vanilla in a small bowl. Add more milk, if needed, until you get a smooth, easy-to-drizzle mixture. Drizzle over the top. Cut into 20 bars.

Food processor method: You do not have to wash the bowl of the processor between steps. Combine ingredients for the bottom layer with a few pulses until crumbly. Pack in pan. Bake as above. Prepare topping in the processor in the same way. Place in a bowl and set aside. Then, place brown sugar, eggs and vanilla in processor bowl and process until blended. Add dry ingredients and pulse a few times. Stir in raisins. Continue as above.

Yield: 70 brownies

1 cup flour

¾ cup Dutch process cocoa, see note

½ teaspoon baking powder

¼ teaspoon salt

2 cups sugar

2 sticks (1 cup) unsalted butter, melted

2 teaspoons vanilla

4 eggs

1 cup coarsely chopped walnuts, plus 70 walnut halves

2 packages (20 ounces each) chocolate-flavored almond bark, see note

Prep time: 35 minutes

Bake time: 35 minutes per batch

Uptown Brownies

1. Heat oven to 350 degrees. Sift together flour, cocoa, baking powder and salt in a medium bowl; set aside. Beat sugar, butter and vanilla with a mixer on medium-high speed; add eggs. Add flour mixture slowly to creamy mixture. Fold in chopped nuts.

2. Transfer batter to a 13-by-9-inch pan sprayed with cooking spray. Spread mixture over pan, smoothing out the top with a spatula. Bake until puffed and brown, about 35 minutes. Cool completely in pan. Cut ½ inch off the edges to create an even edge; discard. Cut into 1-inch squares; set aside.

3. Melt the almond bark in a medium saucepan over low heat. Line a baking sheet with wax paper. Pierce the bottom of a brownie with a fork to attach firmly; dip the brownie into the melted chocolate to coat the top and sides. Lift the brownie out of the chocolate; top with a walnut half. To remove from fork, set bottom edge of brownie onto wax paper, gently pushing on top of the nut while pulling out fork. Let cool on wax paper to harden.

Note: Dutch process cocoa is darker in color with a smoother, richer flavor than traditional cocoa. Chocolate-flavored almond bark is sold in supermarket baking sections.

This rich chocolate brownie from Mary DiCarlo earned an honorable mention in the 2004 contest. DiCarlo created the recipe as a novelty to sell at a fundraiser and described the treats as **"no ordinary suburban brownie."**

Taking home the top prize in 2011, Cindy Beberman created a recipe in which hazelnut-studded fingers with orange zest are **dipped and drizzled in two different chocolates.** Beberman likes the sheen that the paraffin gives to the chocolate, but you can omit if you like. She also said to bring the cookies to room temperature before serving.

Yield: 4 dozen cookies

Hazelnut Orange Fingers in Chocolate

1½ cups shelled whole raw hazelnuts

1 cup unsalted butter, softened but still firm to touch

½ cup superfine sugar, see note

2 teaspoons vanilla

½ teaspoon salt, rounded

Zest from 4 clementines or 1 tablespoon orange zest

2 cups flour

12 ounces dark or semisweet chocolate morsels, or chopped

½ ounce paraffin, about 1 square inch

6 ounces milk chocolate morsels, or chopped

Prep time: 75 minutes

Bake time: 15 minutes per batch

Freeze time: 45 minutes

Note: Instead of buying superfine sugar, you can process granulated sugar a few seconds in a food processor.

1. Heat oven to 350 degrees. Spread hazelnuts on baking sheet; toast until golden brown and fragrant, 13 to 14 minutes. Cool a few minutes; while still warm, rub briskly in clean towel to remove most of the skins. Place cooled nuts in a food processor; process until finely ground but not yet powder.

2. Beat butter on medium to high speed in bowl of electric mixer, 30 seconds. Add sugar, salt, vanilla and zest; beat until light and fluffy. Add nuts; beat well. Add flour; mix on slow just until well combined.

3. Roll a tablespoon of dough between your palms, forming dough into finger shapes about 2 inches long. Place on large parchment-lined or ungreased baking sheet, 2 inches apart. Bake until outer cookies are just turning golden on the tips, 15 minutes. Cool 1 minute on baking sheet; transfer to wire rack to finish cooling. Place in freezer to chill.

4. Meanwhile, melt dark chocolate and paraffin in double boiler over barely simmering water (or in heavy saucepan over low heat), stirring constantly until smooth; remove from heat. Pour into a glass measuring cup; set cup in pan of hot water so chocolate remains fluid. Dip half of cookie into chocolate; gently shake off excess. Let set up for a moment; place on wax paper-lined cookie sheets. Place in freezer until chocolate is set, about 15 minutes.

5. Melt milk chocolate in a small heavy saucepan over low heat (or in microwave according to package directions), stirring constantly until smooth. With a spoon, drizzle thin lines of milk chocolate in decorative manner over chilled cookies. (We also like a small squeeze bottle for this.) Return to freezer to set, about 15 minutes.

Yield: 4 dozen bars

John's Cocoa Nutty Bars

In 2008, when he was only 10 years old, John Manos earned an honorable mention for this recipe, which yields a rich bar cookie with peanut butter and chocolate icing. Note: Natural peanut butter does not work here.

3	cups semisweet chocolate chips
¾	cup butter cut into tablespoons
1½	cups flour
¾	cup unsweetened cocoa powder
½	teaspoon baking powder
½	teaspoon salt
4	large eggs
1½	cups sugar
2	teaspoons vanilla
¾	cup creamy peanut butter, see note
½–⅔	cups chopped peanuts

Prep time: 25 minutes

Bake time: 12 to 15 minutes per batch

Cool time: 20 minutes

1. Heat oven to 375 degrees. Melt 1½ cups of the chocolate chips and the butter in a large saucepan over low heat, stirring constantly; let cool. Combine the flour, cocoa powder, baking powder and salt in small bowl; set aside.

2. Beat the eggs, sugar and vanilla in a large bowl with a mixer on medium speed until combined; gradually add the dry ingredients, beating well. Add the reserved chocolate mixture; beat well. Spread the dough onto a greased 15-by-10-inch rimmed baking sheet; bake until firm, about 12 to 15 minutes. Cool until barely warm, about 20 minutes.

3. Spread the peanut butter over the chocolate layer; sprinkle with the peanuts. Melt the remaining 1½ cups of the chocolate chips; spread while warm over the nut layer. Let cool completely; cut into squares.

Note: Sue Manos said she microwaves the peanut butter for 5 to 10 seconds to soften it for spreading.

Butter Crumb Cheesecake Cookies

Ellen Monaghan won third place in 2011 for this luscious tri-layer number. She said her tweaked-over-the-years recipe was one of her "happiest accidents ever," and every time she makes these, part of her "is a giddy little six-year-old, in an oversized apron, standing tippy-toed beside [her] mom."

⅓ cup unsalted butter, softened

⅓ cup packed brown sugar

1 cup flour

½ cup chopped walnuts

¼ cup granulated sugar

1 package (8 ounces) cream cheese, softened

1 egg

1 tablespoon fresh lemon juice

½ teaspoon vanilla

🕐 **Prep time:** 15 minutes

Bake time: 37 to 40 minutes per batch

1. Heat oven to 350 degrees. Cream butter and brown sugar together with an electric mixer in a bowl. Add flour and walnuts. Mix to make a crumb mixture. Reserve 1 cup for topping. Press remainder into bottom of an 8-inch-square pan sprayed lightly with cooking spray. Bake until lightly browned, 12 to 15 minutes. Remove from oven; cool on cooling rack.

2. Meanwhile, beat granulated sugar with cream cheese in a bowl until smooth. Add egg, lemon juice and vanilla. Beat until smooth. Spread mixture over cooled crust; sprinkle reserved crumb mixture over top. Bake, 25 minutes. Cool completely on rack before cutting into bars about 1¼ inch square.

Grandma Grump's Peanut Butter Drizzles

Meme Baynes won second place in 2006 for these bar cookies, which she described as a family favorite. Baynes recalled driving around with her father when she was a girl, delivering packages of her mother's homemade cookies to family and friends.

Cookie base:

2   cups flour

2   cups quick-cooking oats

1   teaspoon baking soda

½   teaspoon salt

2   sticks (1 cup) butter, softened

1   cup granulated sugar

1   cup packed light brown sugar

2   eggs

⅔   cup creamy peanut butter

1   teaspoon vanilla

1   package (12 ounces) semisweet chocolate chips

Topping:

1   cup confectioners' sugar

½   cup creamy peanut butter

¼   cup whipping cream or milk

Prep time: 25 minutes

Bake time: 20 to 25 minutes per batch

1. Heat oven to 350 degrees. For the cookie base, stir together the flour, oats, baking soda and salt in a large bowl; set aside. Beat together the butter and sugars with a mixer on medium speed until fluffy; add the eggs, beating until combined. Add peanut butter and vanilla; beat until smooth. Stir in the flour-oat mixture, 1 cup at a time.

2. Press dough into a 15-by-10-inch jellyroll pan; bake until firm and beginning to brown, 20 to 25 minutes. Meanwhile, for topping, stir together confectioners' sugar, peanut butter and cream in a small bowl; set aside.

3. Remove cookie base from oven; sprinkle with the chocolate chips. Spread chocolate over entire sheet as it melts. (If chocolate chips don't melt completely, return pan to oven for 30 seconds.) Drizzle the topping over the chocolate. Place pan on a rack to cool completely. Cut into 1½-by-1-inch bars.

From top: Cranberry-Swirled White Chocolate Cheesecake Bars (p. 205); Laced Cookies (p. 177); Toffee Mandelscotti (opposite)

Yield: About 3 dozen cookies

Toffee Mandelscotti

Gail E. Aranoff described these cookies, for which she earned second place in 2001, as a hybrid of the Jewish mandelbrot she grew up eating and the Italian biscotti of her next-door neighbor. She suggested sprinkling them with raw sugar or dipping the ends in chocolate, then rolling them in chopped hazelnuts for an extra-festive touch.

3 eggs
1 cup vegetable oil
1 cup sugar
1 teaspoon vanilla
3½ cups flour
1 teaspoon baking powder
1 teaspoon salt
1 bag (12 ounces) semi-sweet chocolate chips
8 ounces almond toffee bits

Prep time: 20 minutes

Chill time: 3 hours

Bake time: 45 minutes per batch

1. Place eggs, oil, sugar and vanilla in the bowl of an electric mixer. Beat until light in color, 5 minutes. Sift together flour, baking powder and salt. Mix into eggs just until incorporated. Do not overmix. Stir in chocolate chips and toffee bits. Wrap dough in plastic wrap. Refrigerate 3 hours.

2. Heat oven to 350 degrees. Divide dough into 4 pieces; shape each piece into 8-by-3-inch logs on an ungreased cookie sheet. Bake until lightly browned, 25 minutes.

3. Reduce oven to 300 degrees. Remove cookie logs from baking sheet; cut diagonally into ¾-inch slices. Place sliced cookies back on baking sheet. Bake until golden brown, 20 minutes.

Penny Scorzo McGrath's Double Chocolate Walnut Biscotti

This biscotti earned Penny Scorzo McGrath an honorable mention in 2010. The recipe was adapted from the December 1994 issue of *Gourmet* magazine, via Epicurious.com.

2 cups flour

½ cup unsweetened cocoa powder

1 teaspoon baking soda

1 teaspoon salt

¾ stick unsalted butter, softened

1 cup sugar

2 eggs

1 cup walnuts, chopped

¾ cup semisweet chocolate chips

1 tablespoon confectioners' sugar

Prep time: 25 minutes

Bake time: 54 minutes per batch

1. Heat oven to 350 degrees. Whisk together flour, cocoa powder, baking soda and salt in a medium bowl; set aside. Beat together butter and sugar in a large bowl with mixer until light and fluffy. Beat in eggs, one at a time. Stir in flour mixture to form a stiff dough. Stir in walnuts and chocolate chips.

2. Form dough into two slightly flattened logs, each 12 inches long and 2 to 3 inches wide, on a buttered, floured large baking sheet. Sprinkle logs with confectioners' sugar. Bake until slightly firm to the touch, 35 minutes. Cool logs on baking sheet 5 minutes.

3. Cut logs diagonally into ¾-inch slices on a cutting board. Arrange biscotti, cut sides down, on baking sheet. Bake until crisp, about 19 minutes. Transfer to a wire rack to cool.

SOURCES

This book was created from the following sources:

Stevens, Heidi. "Sweet visions." Wednesday, December 4, 2013.

Gray, Joe. "Editor's pick: One more cookie." Wednesday, December 12, 2012.

Stevens, Heidi. "Sweets of the season." Wednesday, November 28, 2012.

Mahany, Barbara. "A little bit of magic." Wednesday, November 30, 2011.

Daley, Bill. "Chocolate indulgence." Wednesday, December 1, 2010.

Mahany, Barbara. "Pressed into our hearts." Wednesday, December 1, 2010.

Mahany, Barbara. "Every cookie has a story." Wednesday, December 2, 2009.

Nunn, Emily. "Star power." Wednesday, December 3, 2008.

Pierce, Donna. "Sweet victory." Wednesday, November 28, 2007.

Pierce, Donna. "Comfort and joy." Wednesday, November 29, 2006.

Pierce, Donna. "Sweet discoveries." Wednesday, November 30, 2005.

Pierce, Donna. "Sweet expressions." Wednesday, December 1, 2004.

Eddy, Kristin. "Crunch time." Wednesday, December 17, 2003.

Pierce, Donna. "A gift of memories." Wednesday, December 3, 2003.

Pierce, Donna. "Sweet memories." Wednesday, December 4, 2002.

Eddy, Kristin. "Tiny treasures." Wednesday, December 28, 2001.

Rice, William. "Edible heirlooms." Wednesday, November 29, 2000.

Rice, William. "Tastes of tradition." Wednesday, December 2, 1998.

Eddy, Kristin. "Sweet victory." Wednesday, December 3, 1997.

Haddix, Carol Mighton. "Sweet reflections." Wednesday, December 4, 1996.

Dailey, Pat. "Sweet success stories." Wednesday, December 6, 1995.

Brownson, JeanMarie. "Winning traditions." Thursday, December 8, 1994.

Brownson, JeanMarie. "Season of spice." Thursday, December 2, 1993.

Sidebar. "Cookies delight 4 generations." Thursday, December 3, 1992.

Sullivan, Barbara. "3 cookie champs." Thursday, December 3, 1992.

Brownson, JeanMarie. "Reaching for the stars." Thursday, December 5, 1991.

Sidebar. "Crescents are a century old." Thursday, December 13, 1990.

Van Matre, Lynn. "Cookie carols." Thursday, December 13, 1990.

Chang, Iris. "Adding memories to sugar and flour, 3 bakers top 500 entries." Thursday, December 14, 1989.

Hevrdejs, Judy. "Sugar, flour, butter & love." Thursday, December 8, 1988.

PHOTO CREDITS

CONTEST WINNERS BY YEAR

• First place   • Second place   • Third place

INDEX